HEALING
THE MALE SOUL

HEALING THE MALE SOUL

◆ ||| ◆ ||| ◆

Christianity and the Mythic Journey

◆

DWIGHT H. JUDY

Illustrations by Nancy Rosser Hutchins

CROSSROAD · NEW YORK

1992
The Crossroad Publishing Company
370 Lexington Avenue, New York, NY 10017

Printed in the United States of America

Library of Congress Cataloging-in-Publication Data

Judy, Dwight H.
    Healing the male soul : Christianity and the mythic journey /
Dwight H. Judy ; illustrations by Nancy Rosser Hutchins.
        p.   cm.
    Includes bibliographical references.
    ISBN 0-8245-1199-9 (hard)
        1. Men—Psychology.   2. Men—Religious life.   3. Masculinity
(Psychology)   4. Mythology—Psychological aspects.   5. Christianity—
Psychology.   I. Title.
BF692.5.J83   1992; aa21 08-20-92
248.8′42—dc20   92-29727
                                                                CIP

For my sons, Joseph and Daniel

CONTENTS

ACKNOWLEDGMENTS

At the beginning of this quest for the roots of the Western male soul, I wish to acknowledge the many contributors to this task. It could not have been undertaken without the scholarship of Erich Neumann, Ken Wilber, and Julian Jaynes, who laid the foundation for drawing on resources from mythology and sacred story to construct a history of human consciousness. Without the collections of mythic and religious sources of Joseph Campbell and Mircea Eliade, this task would have been equally impossible. And, of course, a great debt of gratitude goes to Carl Jung, in his reawakening of the Western mind to the deep underlying collective stories that inform our existence.

This work was equally dependent on individuals who have contributed their support and understanding to me directly. My original research on this project was directed by June Singer during my doctoral studies at the Institute of Transpersonal Psychology. Without her encouragement, I might not have ventured into this arena of study, where myth, sacred story, and personal experience blend to enhance our current life-understandings. There are many men who in their relationships with me, past and present, also have contributed to the developing understandings of this work. Though too numerous to name, I acknowledge each one. Many have graciously allowed some inclusion of their inner experiences in this book. I especially offer my appreciation to the men and boys with whom I have lived most closely, my father, my brother, my two sons, my grandfather, and my father-in-law. A very important word must also be expressed to the significant women who have shaped my existence so profoundly, my wife, Ruth, my mother, my grandmother, my mother-in-law, and the many women it has been my priviledge to know as coworkers, and various companions along the way.

This project has taken many years to bring to completion, and I want to offer appreciation to my literary agent, John White, who encouraged me in this project for many years, and to my editor at Crossroad, Bob Heller, who helped me shape the final stage of writing. I also express my appreciation to Nancy Rosser Hutchins, whose illustrations enliven the text.

In 1980 I left my life as a parish minister to undertake a study leave. I knew that the time had come for a deeper understanding of self and God. What I discovered surprised me. Side by side in my inner world, ancient warriors, who seemed imbedded in my body's pain, and a radiant Christ, who conveyed my life's vision, emerged during this time of interior awakening. The tasks of the last decade took me not only into the arena of internal challenges but also of external challenges, as I then sought to bring this awakened inner life into meaningful public service. It is not yet an easy time for the exponents of the inner life to find a niche in our culture. Yet, now that the arduous years of developing new structure through which to convey these understandings are past, I would not have wished it otherwise. For in the years of creating a new faculty post at the Institute of Transpersonal Psychology, in the years of achieving psychologist licensure, in the years of taking the inner life processes back into the church through many retreat opportunities, fortitude has been awakened. The male soul has thrived on challenge throughout the centuries. Without that challenge we find ourselves with weakened capacity for service. I invite each reader into a profound willingness to serve this age, in its many needs, with reawakened courage, vision, love, and fortitude.

1

♦ ♦ ♦

BEGINNING THE JOURNEY

The era of masculine ascendency is ending. While the domination of men in places of power is still evident, the human heart in both men and women is changing. We see the evidence for this change in the burgeoning library of books on women's studies, the concern for human rights and release from dictatorial regimes around the world, and in the inner recesses of the human spirit, where the feminine aspects of God are once again being discovered. Whether we look at political, family, psychological, or theological concerns, there is a changing face to the human story, a face with more prominence given to women than fifty or one hundred years ago.

At such a time of ending, it is important to trace some perspective on the past, so that we chart the future with wisdom. The recent development of interest in men in discovering a deeper masculinity, particularly through the interest generated by Robert Bly's focus on Iron John, has the ring of other first steps toward consciousness of identified minorities. Western man, for the first time since his ascendency, now realizes that he is a minority in the world's population. While he maintains much political and social dominance, Western man finds himself in a new wasteland. Suddenly, he is beginning to realize that he is not the center of the human story. The center is shifting. When Western man was the dominant force in the world, he did not need to reflect so consciously on himself, but now he begins to see that his story is only one of the stories shaping the human story. Like other identifiable groups in our time, Western man needs to find his own cultural roots, the origins of his current loves, hates, hopes, and disappointments. In a time of such monumental change it is important and appropriate to reach for deeper roots of identity.

It is extremely difficult while within such a cosmic or universal change process to comment accurately on what is happening. Yet we must attempt to point in a direction to satisfy our curiosity and to assist us in our decision processes. What I hope to do in *Healing the Male Soul* is to point a direction toward understanding the current change in self-understanding and relationships between men and women through the perspective of the history of human consciousness. This perspective is relatively new as a way of understanding the human story. It can be an enormously helpful perspective within which to view the development of Christianity and changes in the psychological self-understanding of Western humanity through the centuries.

The quest for the male soul has been a very personal story for me, as well. I grew up in the age of scientific materialism, under the shadow of the atomic bomb. As I entered junior high school, the United States was struggling with its inferiority complex over the launching of the first satellite, "Sputnik," by the U.S.S.R. It was a time in which the aim of our national policy seemed to be to turn every youth into an engineer or scientist. As a child with a quick mind able to comprehend the math and science taught me, but with a heart inclined more toward religion than science, it was not an easy time. I learned the rational method well. I learned to doubt my intuitions and to distance myself from my body. As I have reflected on my late adolescence, I think that my contact with my own religious feelings and my feeling nature was kept alive primarily through music. I remember vividly receiving flashes of insight during concerts. Classical music was my prayer, although I did not know it at the time.

By my early thirties, the unexplored parts of myself could no longer be ignored. My dream life awakened from a slumber of many years. The sensuality and sexuality of my body cried out for more attention. I was most fortunate to have married a woman who could go with me through my changes and who knew how cut off I was from my awareness of my darker emotions and many deeper motivations. For almost ten years I had served as a pastor, weekly immersing myself in scripture, daily living with people in their illnesses, deaths, divorces, celebrations, and joys. Yet the time had come for a deeper discovery of God and self.

Much to my surprise, in this era when I devoted so much energy to my own psychological development in my early to mid-thirties,

I found myself suddenly having inner visions of ancient warriors. I, who had made a lifelong commitment to pacifism, found myself now also understanding that the battlefield had been a place of transcendence for the warriors of history. I had long known that the "warrior of righteousness," who worked arduously to better the world through nonviolent means in social action, was a deep and vibrant part of myself. This warrior of righteousness, I found, was kin to the historical warriors of battle. I found the darker side of the warrior as well In an extended meditation retreat, I found the story unfolding in my mind of a medieval crusader going off to battle filled with the love of Christ. When he began to experience combat, however, he discovered that he had fallen in love with killing, plunder, rape, and pillage. He didn't realize until he was dying, himself a victim of battle, how far he had strayed from his original love of Christ. This, and other meditation experiences, made me aware of the need to understand within myself the role of the warrior in male psychology, its boons and its demons, and how these might still be unconsciously shaping us.

What was most clear to me was my own split between mind and body and the need to bring fully into consciousness my neglected aspects of physical life and emotional awareness. I felt like a classic victim of the Western tendency to split mind and body. It was now time to mend and heal this split. It was time to make a deeper passage into self. Through that era of my life in the early 1980s, I was exposed to transpersonal and Jungian psychology, group dynamics, spiritual practices from many traditions, bioenergetic breathwork, and other forms of bodywork. I plunged headlong into an inner journey that in fact did heal the split between body and mind, between feelings and expression, and that opened an interior region of spiritual awareness to me that I had longed to know but felt might forever be lost to people in our time.

Healing the Male Soul is my offering to the current thinking on male psychology. It is a historical answer to the problem of the Western split between mind and body. From the perspective of the history of human consciousness, it is clear that with the origins of written language a major change was taking place in the mind of humanity. It seems clear from this perspective that although humanoid species have been present on the earth for one to two million years, the rise of modern consciousness, as we know it, with a distinction among the functions of feelings, rational thoughts, imagination, intuition, and sensory awareness, has not been present for all of that time. Instead it arises with the development of written language. For the West, the most dramatic period of this development occurs concurrently with the rise of Greek philosophy and Hebrew scripture approximately one thousand years before Christ. The stories of the Hebrew Patriarchs reach back through oral tradition into the second millennium B.C.E., but begin to be woven together into the Pentateuch as a written document around 500 B.C.E. (Blair 1975). This is the same era as Buddha in India and Lao Tzu in China. Clearly, in the millennium before Christ a great shift was taking place in human awareness, a development laying the foundation for contemporary consciousness. The roots, however, of our inner drives and distresses reach much further back than this era.

It is fascinating to try to stand back and take in these facts. Humanity in some form has been on the earth for one to two million years. The record of written language and philosophical and religious discourse as we know it is but the "blink" of an eye in this time frame. Thus, when I sought to delve into the origins of the Western split between body and mind, I found myself tracing mythic record and the oral tradition recorded in scripture and in Greek mythology. These sources enable us to venture further back into human history than we are able otherwise to go, because the stories they record were passed from generation to generation prior to written language.

Western consciousness was birthed in the Middle East and Mediterranean worlds two thousand to four thousand years ago. That era brought together the oral traditions of mythologies that became the stories of the Greek and Roman religions and the stories that became the basis of the Hebrew scriptures. It is very helpful to realize that our Judeo-Christian scriptures are a patchwork of oral tradition and direct writing. Scripture contains oral tradition that reaches back beyond the time it was written down, such as the stories of the Patriarchs, and it contains direct writings, such as those of Paul. We thus have within scripture some material that is similar in origin to Greek mythology, such as the story of creation, the Garden of Eden, the flood, Abraham, and the other Patriarchs. At the same time, we have other writings, such as Ecclesiastes, that are much more like the philosophers of the Hellenic world. Throughout scripture, we find this rich patchwork and thus an enormously fertile ground for the study of the development of moral and religious thought for a thousand years.

The framework with which I will explore the male soul and its contemporary split between mind and body will thus take us into the era of prehistory. It will draw heavily on both Greek mythology and on Judeo-Christian scripture. Both of these sources contribute to the unfolding and development of Western thought. The origins of our collective history involve both sources.

There is no final word on these issues, of course, except the one that each man is writing with his own life and thought. My hope in this writing is thus to inspire as well as to inform. I invite you into a journey into Western male consciousness that I hope will illumine your own journey into self and journey into God.

I have chosen the term "journey" with care. This exploration is more of a journey than a final statement on male concerns. Within a journey, it is as important to be involved on the trip itself as it is to find the final destination. This particular journey does not have an outward but rather an inward destination. If it is successful, it will take you more deeply into yourself. It will be a journey that I hope will be as meaningful for women as for men. I hope that it will help us as men and as those who relate to men to understand male psychology better. I hope that men will be able to find some iden-tifying perspectives for their lives, and that women will find help in better understanding the significant men in their lives. But I also intend that this journey might illumine the "masculine principle" within women and find a significance for women's self-discovery of many parts of themselves. A great promise of the time of change in which we live is that we may begin to see one another beyond the sex roles of the past and honor the deep feminine and masculine within each person.

Jacob: A Glimpse of the Journey

Many stories in scripture might be used to demonstrate the type of journey into the male soul that we will make together. Jacob, however, stands out as a prime example of the capacity for ancient story to elicit deeper self-understanding. This "glimpse" or preview will prepare us for the more involved journey to come.

The story of Jacob has many substories, not unlike the stages of our life. There is the story of his birth as he comes forth grasping the heel of his brother Esau. There is the story of his robbing his brother Esau of his birthright as firstborn, through the complicity of his mother. At that point, we will pick up the story with more details.

Once he has received the birthright and his dying father's blessing, Jacob flees. He must leave all behind. He has gained the blessing to lose everything it might have meant to him. He must face a desolated wilderness alone. In the midst of his wilderness experience, when everything is totally lost to him, he receives a dream/vision from God of angels ascending and descending between earth and heaven, the vision known as Jacob's ladder. Within that vision, he finds the courage to go on into the unknown.

He comes to a new land and there he learns to give his heart to a woman, Rachel. He agrees to labor for her father, Laban, for seven years in order to win her hand in marriage. Through the trickery of Laban, however, he is given Rachel's sister Leah on his wedding night. Now, he agrees to labor another seven years for Rachel. During this first labor, he thought he was fulfilling his heart's desire, only to find that he had been fulfilling Laban's plan instead. During the second seven years, however, he labors and wins his heart's desire in Rachel. At the end of fourteen years, he has developed a very large family, and he could have left the service of Laban. Instead, he decides to labor seven years for himself. During this time he builds up his herds and his wealth. He works to increase his wealth using the trickery that is natural to him. He is very successful.

Yet his heart is heavy. His past wrong to Esau troubles him. He decides that he must journey home to reconcile himself to Esau. He takes his vast herds and family with him and sets out. As he approaches the land of Esau, he sends offerings of his herds before him, hoping to appease Esau's anger. As he prepares to meet Esau face to face, in the night, alone, he wrestles with the angel or with God. Jacob refuses to let the angel go until he blesses him. At last, he is told: you will no longer be called Jacob (which means grabber), but you will be called Israel, which means "he strove with God and man and prevailed." But Jacob will limp for the rest of his life from this encounter.

Finally, Jacob meets Esau, and the brothers embrace. Esau has forgiven Jacob long ago, so much so that Esau was puzzled by the herds that Jacob had sent before him. Another saga unfolds then for Jacob as the father of Joseph.

Jacob stands at a profound point in Western culture. Jacob is given the name Israel, because he strove with God and man and prevailed. I want to suggest that this image of striving with and against reality, striving to create one's own world in the face of enormous odds, is a hallmark of the Western male soul. This energy to struggle and create new worlds is the dynamic energy of the masculine principle. In the very fabric of the early Hebrew concepts of human life, this principle is given the place of greatest honor. Thus, to be a man, to be Israel, is to be one who is ready to struggle with life and to be cocreator of human society and the world with God.

We find similar images throughout scripture. Moses exerts enormous personal authority to lead the people out of slavery in Egypt and to gain the vision of the new society given in the Ten Commandments. In the story of Job, we find that the great voice out of the whirlwind will finally talk directly to Job only when he gets up off his dungheap and "stands up like a man." Abraham will be blessed if he will leave everything behind and journey forth into a new and unknown land. God the creator stands behind the commands, images, and tasks. Western man must learn to stand on his own, to create new worlds, and to strive even with God.

We find in Jacob several of the tasks that each man must journey for himself. We find the task of leaving home, taking blessing with us. We find the task of braving the wilderness alone. We find the task of finding the mature love of a woman. We find the task of struggling with the older masculine, as Jacob struggles for what is rightfully his from Laban. We find the task of making one's own creative contribution to culture. And we find the task of making peace with God.

As we expand on these tasks of masculine consciousness, the tasks that every man must face, we will find them illuminated by many other stories. In general, Jacob's tasks outline the tasks of mature manhood. However, I would state the more general framework of the tasks of masculine consciousness derived from the record of myth and sacred story to be the following:

1. Leaving home and separating from our mothers. We will see this theme illustrated in the awakening of modern consciousness,

two thousand to four thousand years ago, in its separation from the Great Mother religions. This theme will be played out in each of our lives as the separation and differentiation from our families, our mothers, and from nature.

2. Developing ego strength in contest with the world of men, including the struggle for separation and equality with our fathers. This is the birth of the masculine through the principles we will discover in the hero-warrior.

3. Going to the wilderness, developing deeper soul through contests in the interior world. This deeper insight comes to Jacob in his times alone when God breaks through in the wilderness. It is the domain of the principle of masculine consciousness we will call the hero-transcendent.

4. Encountering woman, with the tasks of discerning the love of woman as companion and friend, separating our own internalized images of the feminine from our relationships with our wives, mothers, and other women whom we love and with whom we work. These are enormous tasks that must be worked out in relationship, as Jacob does in his relationships with his mother, Rachel, and Leah. We will find this theme illuminated in the stories of the Holy Grail.

5. Encountering man, working out our relationship to the deep masculine, wresting power from the older generation of men, finding companionship with our contemporary generation of men, making peace with our fathers. These tasks we must finally approach directly as Jacob did in his relationship with Laban and Esau. We find different perspectives on this theme through all of the sagas we will explore but especially in the relationships between men in the stories of the Holy Grail.

6. Encountering God, wrestling out together the visions of creative service to the world. This image predominates the task of the hero-creative, given birth in the Hebrew Partiarchs and in the life of Jesus, and given fresh insights in the stories of the Holy Grail. This theme is very much alive in our time, in the stories we are each writing in our own lifetime.

As we make this journey into the male soul, we will begin with an exploration of the process of story, as it relates to our own self-understanding. We will then explore these predominant themes: the hero-warrior, the hero-transcendent, and the hero-creative. Along the way we will seek an understanding of the six tasks of mature manhood, engaging our own life stories with many stories of our cultural heritage. We will journey into the stories of Hercules and Dionysus. We will visit again with Jacob. We will speak of Jesus, Paul, Augustine, and the monastics of early Christianity. We will explore elements of the stories of the Holy Grail, finding the intriguing persons of Parsifal, Gawain, the Fisher King, and the Loathly Damsel. Let us begin with a fresh understanding of the power of story to shape our lives.

Once upon a Time

Once upon a time, humankind understood its life and existence through mythic stories, stories in which human beings struggled with demons and dragons, beasts and gods to lay claim to their rightful place in earthly existence. Such stories abound with tales of capriciousness on the part of gods and humans alike. They form the pattern of meaning which still unconsciously shapes our relationship to reality. For example, we see the roots of human guilt not only in the story of the expulsion of Adam and Eve from the Garden of Eden, but also in the punishment of Prometheus for bringing fire to humanity. We witness the human struggle for authority over nature in the tales of Hercules and the human quest for divine guidance in the stories of Ezekiel, Jonah, and Jesus. We find men seeking creative service through love and work in Parsifal and Jacob.

We are privileged to live in a time of attention to mythic story as a primary route to self-understanding. It seems to me to be no accident that Joseph Campbell came to such prominence near the end of his life. Our contemporary culture is starved for story, for meaningful story, for story that provides a transcendent glimpse into ourselves. Before humankind began to reason about life, to create philosophy and science, humankind told stories about life. Through these stories, preserved in the world's mythologies and scriptures, we glimpse humankind's first conscious attempts to make sense out of its existence. These mythic stories thus take us beyond our current era of written knowledge back into prehistory. They are the living link with our ancestral struggles to create patterns of meaning within our lives.

This story-making quality of the human psyche is still extremely important to us. Whenever we introduce ourselves to another person, we may begin with a few brief descriptions of our work and our family, but before long we are telling stories about ourselves. As we develop intimacy with another person, we share stories of our past, stories that illustrate our fears, our struggles, and our victories. We may even reveal our secret stories, the guarded parts of our past, that come to light only when we have built profound trust. We fantasize about the future in stories as well. When we try to project ourselves forward in time, we will do so in images that contain a story.

The storytelling, myth-making part of the psyche is also the source of our dreams each night. Each dream is like a mystery tale, which can be unraveled to give us a fresh perspective on our inner drives, hopes, fears, and longings. This same myth-making, story-telling part of ourselves has created the collective dreams that we have preserved as mythic and scriptural stories. Like our dreams, these mythic stories are most meaningful when we reflect our conscious awareness upon them.

We are accustomed to applying this approach to the stories of sacred scriptures, if we are a part of a practicing religious tradition. In Judeo-Christian tradition, we are accustomed to reflecting our own life-stories against the stories of those men and women recorded in scripture. Many of us have been highly influenced consciously and unconsciously by the predominant theme of this tradition: namely, that one human being can be in direct relationship with God and can receive meaning and purpose from listening for a direct summons to particular tasks. We may live our lives searching for that "call" and living it out.

For the purposes of this venture into the male soul, I will be using stories from scripture and stories from mythology in the same way. In general, when I speak of sacred story, I will be referring to stories from Judeo-Christian scripture. When I speak of mythic story, I will be referring to Greek mythology and the stories of the Holy Grail. Because I will be weaving a story of the male psyche as contained both in the record of mythology and in scripture, a single type of approach to both bodies of material is useful. Another source of story will be from writers of more contemporary literature. All of these sources will be treated from the perspective of metaphor, providing images through which we can illumine our own personal quest for meaning as contemporary men. What I have attempted to do is to build on research in the history of psychological consciousness through mythology and sacred story. It is a somewhat new genre in psychological literature. It is part history, part psychology, part theology, part mythic story, woven together with much creative imagination. I will work with images addressing the Western male experience. A similar type of story might be written from the sacred texts and mythologies of the East and for women, East and West.

In exploring the patterns of the male psyche as reflected in certain Greek myths, the tales of the Holy Grail, and the Judeo-Christian scriptures, I have suggested three predominant modes or themes and named them the hero-warrior, the hero-transcendent, and the hero-creative. I will treat each theme as a unique character or personality in the saga of male consciousness. Each theme will have its own characteristics, its own stories, and its own gifts and problems to bring to bear for our times. We will see many of our own characteristics as Western men reflected in each of these themes. My thesis is that we must come to terms with each of these as archetypal or underlying patterns within our personalities. They are still very much alive within the male psyche and very much affecting our current life-stories.

The Hero's Journey

The framework within which we will explore the male soul is the hero's journey, as described by Joseph Campbell. From time to time, we will turn to this model for illumination of the mythic patterns we will explore. In *The Hero with a Thousand Faces*, Campbell describes the fundamental pattern of the story of the hero as witnessed in mythology and scriptures of the world's religions. The pattern is shown in Figure 1 (1968a, 245). We will use this model to describe the unique characteristics of each motif: the hero-warrior, the hero-transcendent, and the hero-creative. Each one can be seen to have its own story through this framework.

The cycle begins at the call to adventure. Here the hero is called away from ordinary existence. This is the call of God to Abraham to go to a new land. It is the departure of Jacob from his known land because of the theft of Esau's birthright. The call to adventure to humanity in the Bible is issued as the expulsion of Adam and Eve from the Garden of Eden. The hero or heroine then begins a journey into new territory, whether of the inner or the outer world. There

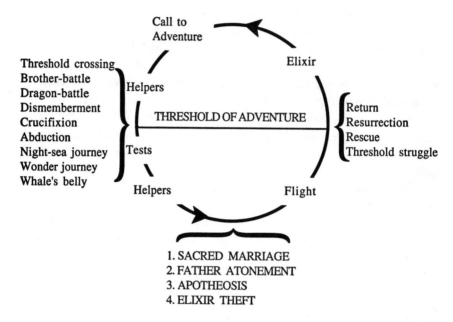

Fig. 1. Reproduced by permission of the publisher from Joseph Campbell, *The Hero with a Thousand Faces* (Princeton, N.J.: Princeton University Press, Bollingen Foundation, Inc., 1949; second edition 1968), p. 245.

is a threshold crossing where everything is left behind. Often accompanying this threshold are great struggles and conflicts. In our personal lives, the threshold is that experience of wilderness in which we have left behind an old job, relationship, task, or home, and have thus lost our moorings. The new forms of stability have not yet manifested for us. In the mythic and sacred stories, these thresholds often hold great threat, as demonstrated in the types of experience associated with the threshold on the chart. Once one has set out on the adventure, there are both tests and helpers. We see one of Jacob's great helpers to be his night dream/vision of the ascent and descent of the angels. He knows that his ultimate divine helper is with him. There are many tests for Jacob, the most pronounced being his relationship with Laban.

At the nadir or most profound part of the journey, a prize is attained. As Campbell surveyed mythic and sacred story, he found four major themes emerging: *sacred marriage, father atonement, apotheosis,* and *elixir theft.* Under these themes, we will find many of the prizes of our male quest. Does sacred marriage manifest within us as a marriage between ego and soul? Does it manifest as a visible marriage with our true beloved, as it did for Jacob? Sacred marriage also manifests in the older strains of mythology, in which there is a marriage of the Great Mother with the male consort. How will we come to terms with our relationship with nature, with our mothers, and our own darker passions? These can all be seen as a part of the theme of sacred marriage. For men, this theme will bring forth the many faces of making peace with the feminine.

Father atonement has been the predominant way Western culture has viewed the crucifixion of Jesus. Father atonement also manifests as Abraham's answering the call of God to go to a new land. It manifests in the hero-warrior's willingness to die under the command of his older male leaders. It manifests personally as making peace with our fathers. This theme has many ramifications for us in making peace with God and in answering the deeper call to meaningful service in our time.

Apotheosis means to become divine. It is a very stong theme in the hero-transcendent. It is the theme of final, full identification with God. The major form this quest has taken in the West is a monastic withdrawal from the world in order to find the deep interior knowledge of God. We will explore the gifts and the problems of this form of spirituality. We can each profit enormously by asking ourselves what form our quest for the divine is taking at the present time. Is it an inward quest? Is it a quest for service to the world? Is it a quest for inner tranquillity? Is it a quest for global peace or ecological balance? How do we envision our approach to God?

Finally, there is a theme that is neglected in our time, yet very significant in mythic story. That is the theme of elixir theft. Jacob is a thief. He comes forth from the womb grabbing after his brother. He steals Esau's blessing. He uses his cunning to make himself wealthy from Laban's herds. Laban, of course, thieves seven years of labor from Jacob. In the fairy tale of Jack and the Beanstalk, Jack thieves back the bag of gold, the goose that lays the golden eggs, and the golden harp. All of these things were his own inheritance. They were his birthright taken by the giant years ago from his father. The theme of theft also manifests when Hercules goes into the underworld to steal back his friend's wife from death. I suggest that this theme is very strong for the hero-creative. The hero-creative is always seeking to bring forth that which is not yet manifest and to bring it into the world of form. This type of thievery, stealing what is actually ours by right and yet which the world is keeping from us, requires great stealth, cunning, ego strength, and perseverence.

After achieving the prize, there is then a return as the hero or heroine seeks to bring the boon back into the ordinary world. There will also be tests and helpers along this pathway. Finally, there is another threshold crossing. One of the common misperceptions of spiritual growth is that because we attain a new insight or deeper knowledge of self, the world will immediately recognize it. Again, Jacob is helpful. His most difficult and profound realization comes at the point of his return. His final test is the wrestling match with God's angel as he nears home. Finally, there is the opportunity to share the elixir for the enrichment of the life of the world. The cycle is completed. For those of us fortunate enough to live many years, there will be a series of such quests, perhaps occurring each decade or so in our lives. This cycle gives us the courage to listen deeply within ourselves to our boredoms, hopes, and dreams, and to take the risk as did Jacob and Abraham to step out again and again into the unknown.

This pattern is so deeply embedded in the human psyche that we see it played out over and over again as the basic model for every Hollywood movie. There is a call to adventure, a desire to create something more out of our lives, that calls to us. We set off on a new quest often toward a prize that we have not yet clearly understood. There are tests and helpers along the way. There is a threshold struggle as we learn to let go of one way of being and struggle to understand the new life that is calling to us. Finally, the boon is achieved. We then begin the cycle of return, which also has its threshold struggle. Finally, there is a return to share the new self-understanding or the new life with the world, to enrich the common story of humanity.

We will each play out this pattern in our own lives in numerous ways. There may, for example, be a major quest that consumes several years. After this quest is complete, we may find ourselves again feeling the restless pull of a new call to adventure. As we explore the themes of the male journey in Western history, we are also invited to keep before us the story of our own lives. It can be illuminating to use the hero's journey model as a way of looking at our lives, seeing the patterns that we play out in different phases and decades. I invite the reader to keep this image before yourself in your exploration. How do the various stories of the hero-warrior, the hero-transcendent, and the hero-creative illumine your journey? Where are you now on the cycle of the hero's journey: at the point of a new call, at the threshold, in the midst of tests and helpers on the way in a new venture, at the point of receiving the boon, at the point of the threshold return, or at the point of giving the elixir back to the world? Perhaps you will find yourself on one cycle with career, another with family, and yet another in your own internal relationship with yourself. Perhaps you will find predominant elements of the hero-warrior, the hero-transcendent, or the hero-creative as you reflect on your journey. Perhaps you will find elements of each. In exercises at the end of each chapter, you will have the opportunity to chart your own quest on the sacred journey of your life, as you reflect on the themes.

As we explore each of the major themes of the male soul, we will look to Campbell's model for understanding. What are the prizes of the hero-warrior, the hero-transcendent, the hero-creative? What tests and helpers appear with each? What gifts do each share with the world and which we can now claim as contemporary men? We will also explore how each theme illuminates the six major tasks of mature manhood described earlier.

The overall pattern of development of the male psyche during the last four thousand years may be illumined through this model. If we look at the whole of the masculine era as one hero's journey, we would see the Fall, as illustrated in mythic story, as the call to adventure. The evidence of mythic history places this development in human consciousness at approximately four thousand years ago. Its antecedents go back into the era of Great Mother worship. We will explore this theme in chapter 2. During the threshold and descent eras on the cycle, male consciousness struggled to differentiate the issues and themes of the hero-warrior and the hero-transcendent, with the hero-warrior predominating. The hero-transcendent predominates approximately one to three thousand years ago, with the dominant figure of Jesus for Western life, and other religious figures of that epoch, such as Buddha and Mohammed. Although the hero-creative is manifest in the early Hebrew tradition of the Patriarchs (Abraham, Jacob, Moses, Joseph, and others), I see the role of the hero-creative contributing most strongly to the human story during the last one thousand years. Presently, the hero-creative is seeking to guide us into the next millen-

A Personal Montage on the Male Soul

When I was ten years old, I traveled with my family to Europe. The year was 1956, only eleven years following World War II. My eyes were opened in that experience to the realities of human suffering and human folly. I experienced the grandeur of European civilization in its palaces, its works of art, and its music. And I experienced the insanity of its wartime destruction. The cathedrals—Florence, St. Peter's, St. Paul's, St. Mark's, each with their rich historical record of saints and persons of power—vied for my attention with the death camps of Hitler's annihilation of the Jews in the name of Aryan purity. Michelangelo's awesome representations of the Renaissance hope for human beauty and physical mastery were counterposed on the remnants of bombed-out cities. The heavily guarded barbed-wire fence and bare earth of the newly lowered Iron Curtain created an ominous prospect for the future.

The tour was sponsored in conjunction with a conference at the World Council of Churches, to which my father was a delegate. The location of the WCC is near Geneva in neutral Switzerland. My family name is Swiss in origin and has a rich history, which we as a family had just begun to discover. A genealogist had just published a volume on the family history, tracing its origin to the ninth century C.E.. The story of my family origin is that a German serf escaped his servitude and made his way into Switzerland where he became established as a landholder and person of some local repute. The name he chose for himself meant "justice." It was a wonderful experience to discover my lost relatives. Here in the first nation to adopt a policy of neutrality, I found pages and pages of persons in the phone book bearing the name, *Tschudin*, one of the Swiss spellings of my name. My name, in its quality of justice earned through difficult effort and sacrifice, contributed to the self-image that struggled toward emergence in my young life, and to which this trip was so significant.

Not only were there such connections with my family's origin, but there were equally strong connections with my religious and cultural origins. Place after place, we toured the points of historical religious significance: at Oxford, the room where John Wesley had lived (founder of the Methodists in the eighteenth century); in Geneva, the monument to the Swiss Reformation leaders, Calvin and

Zwingli; in Rome, St. Peter's and the Vatican, the catacombs and the Colosseum; in Paris, Notre Dame. In Germany, there were conferences with Lutheran church leaders trying to understand the war and renew their nation after it. We attended the *Kirchentag*, a religious festival of some fifty thousand people, gathered as an act of ecumenical renewal. And we visited the death camps of the Nazis where I saw the gas chambers and photographs of the victims and first heard the name of the Christian prisoner martyred in the same atrocities, Dietrich Bonhoeffer. What had happened to the idealism of Christian Germany, the homeland of the Reformation and of the greatest of recent philosophers and theologians, that it had brought forth mass genocide?

While my ten-year-old mind began pondering these questions, my prepubescent body was awakening with the power of awesome warriors. Sculptures in the streets and galleries of powerful nude men at war sent shudders of awakening through me. The honoring, indeed glorifying of the warrior, in paintings such as *The Rape of the Sabine Women*, sent shock waves through my loins. The quintessence of this male power at rest and in beauty was expressed in Michelangelo's *David*. The male's torment left its lasting impression on me in Michelangelo's *Slaves* and in the classical Roman statue *Laocoön*. *Laocoön*, with its central father figure, flanked by two sons, all three in the grip of the serpent monster, has long since haunted me with its expression of the the male's bound state (Figure 3). Other lasting impressions came from Michelangelo's *Pietà*, in which Mary cradles the crucified Christ, and his *Last Judgment* in the Sistine Chapel. I saw in these art works the split I was seeing in wartorn Europe: the awesome, fearful glory of the male in full power, and simultaneously his torment, impotence, and destruction.

Essentially, I have spent my life since that time looking at the world through the question: Why? Why did Europe heap destruction upon itself in this century? Why is it possible for humanity simultaneously to create such awesome beauty and blindly to destroy its creations? Furthermore, is it conceivable to actually consider the possibility of a radical shift in human awareness and action so that the atrocities of war, genocide, and political self-destruction and oppression may become memories of the past? Since childhood, I have believed that this shift can take place. The words of Isaiah and Micah, particularly those promises delivered each Christmas Eve, have profoundly affected me: "They shall beat their swords into

Fig. 3. Laocoön. Marble, height 96″, c. 25 B.C.E., from the Esquiline Hill, Rome. Vatican Museums, Rome.

plowshares; the lion and the lamb shall lie down together, and a little child shall play over the adder's den; nation shall not lift up sword against nation; there shall be peace!" Is it possible to make substantial movement toward this vision for humanity, or must we remain unconsciously paralyzed before the warrior in our midst?

The story to be told is thus intimately involved with the unraveling of my own personal mythology, with those forces that shaped my identity, so catalized in the 1956 European trip. The story to be told, however, is also a collective story, a story of the effects of archetypal forces active in the human psyche for the last four to six thousand years. We are searching for a way to speak of these forces, which are so powerful that they can grip our imaginations, cause nations to sacrifice themselves in war and benevolent causes, and can bring forth both destruction and creativity within our world.

As I read Western history, it is the record of intense struggle between the flesh and the spirit. Western thought has been steeped in this duality. St. Paul admonished the early Christians to subdue the flesh to the spirit (Rom. 6:12–14). In its quest for this spiritual awakening, the Western mind has soared to the heights of rational capability and beyond, into the contemplation of the divine mysteries without form. Yet it has also remained seemingly enslaved to the flesh, exhibiting the most aggressive of political and ecomonic expansion, and the virtual enslavement of the rest of the world to itself through warfare. Thus, by the nineteenth century, all of the world was either directly under European influence or had been viewed as appropriate for European dominance. By what right had the Spanish, Portuguese, Dutch, English, French, Germans, Russians, and their descendants in the New World, the white races of the world, sought domination of the Americas, Africa, India, and laid claims unsuccessfully to the Middle East and to the Orient?

We seek also to understand the creative dynamism of the Western spirit: the creativity that has given us technologies of wondrous powers and the capacity to alter forever the relationship between nature and humankind.

We are seeking to understand three distinct yet intertwining parts of the Western personality: the hero-warrior, the hero-transcendent, and the hero-creative. The hero-warrior and the hero-transcendent have been both at war with each other and cooperating throughout the era of masculine ascendency. They are mirrored in the dynamic of the myths of the brothers or twins, who may battle, kill, or become reconciled to one another. As we will discover in examining the rise of the hero-transcendent, Western spirituality has sought to subdue the flesh and to convert the passions from unbridled aggression in order to allow the rational mind to emerge into maturity. However, this very means of control and containment of the warrior's aggression and passion has created a dissociation with the body's powerful energies that fostered a periodic eruption of the full masculine physical power, driven by unconscious forces. The priests in various eras were all too eager to be part of the Western warrior's expansive drama. Western history has been enslaved to warfare. This phenomenon is by no means limited to the West. It has dominated world politics in many regions of the globe during the era of male ascendency. The task before us, however, is to explore the particularities of the Western problem with the warrior's predominance.

Writing during World War II, Carl Jung wrestled with this problem of Western history. His conclusion was that, although Western culture had the vision of Christian life before it, Christianity had not penetrated into the core of the Western psyche. Instead, in its heart, Western culture remained essentially untouched. "Christian civilization has proved hollow to a terrifying degree: it is all veneer, but the inner man has remained untouched and therefore unchanged" (Jung 1968b, §12). Why has the model of subduing the flesh to the spirit proven inadequate? Why has the beast within humanity continued to plague the earth? The answers to our questions must involve a plunge into the archaic realms. We will need to look for answers not only in our present dilemmas but also in the cultural milieu of ancient history.

The masculine psyche is undergoing a transformation at the present time. This transformation involves us individually and collectively in a deep interior search. To put it simply, we must have a new relationship to spirit and to flesh. The hero-creative, as a reconciling force, must now come into his full potentiality. In Western culture, the spiritual quest became highly identified with the rational function of the mind. And in the effort to subdue the flesh in its attainment, not only were aggressive tendencies inadequately addressed, but feelings of sensitivity were lost as well. The existentialist crisis of the latter part of the twentieth century, together with its theological offspring, "the death of God," can be viewed as evidence that the development of rational thought has reached its zenith. If man is only rational, he finds that he is empty, lonely, cut off from earth and woman, and even from his masculine God, because this God finally demands crucifixion and a dismemberment of egoic rationality to bring us into mystical ecstasy. The shadow side of the rise of rationality dissociated from feeling is evidenced now in the threat of annihilation we are able to pose toward all of the earth. We must claim both the rewards and the emptiness of our achievement and surrender to a fresh renewal of life purpose. This interior shift is mirrored or perhaps even catalyzed by the shift in political, social, and economic power in our time. The rise in self-determination throughout the world and the end to the Cold War have brought us to a new era, wherein old styles of political domination give way to individual and collective creativity in the market-place. The hero-creative must now emerge in full authority to reconcile the hero-warrior and the hero-transcendent and guide us into the next millennium.

Is it possible for the hero now to find a reconciliation with flesh and an awakening of spirit? My hope is that the chaos of this century, with its tremendous upheavals of warfare, together with the nuclear and ecological threat, has begun to move us toward new visions of planetary life. I am hopeful that this change is happening in part because of the willingness of more and more men to open the door of the unconscious and to explore there the dark, archaic, untouched realms as well as the realms of light and compassion. The treasures found there indicate that there are new possibilities emerging out of the collective unconscious to assist us to make the needed transition toward wholeness at this time in human evolution. This shift can be seen in dreams, visions, guided imagery, and spontaneous expressions of new myths. What these images suggest is that the masculine identity, long dissociated between the hero-warrior and the hero-transcendent, may at last be healing itself.

As a child, I lay awake at night with my homemade crystal radio to my ear listening to the the news report that President Eisenhower had sent military advisors to Indo-China, and I prayed, knowing in my tender heart that it was setting our nation on the course of war. The heroes of my childhood were Gandhi and Schweitzer. With growing awe I watched the rise of a living warrior of justice, Martin Luther King, Jr.

I entered college with a thirst for Western culture and history. I was asking the question of why Western civilization had come to the point of self-destruction witnessed in the wars of the twentieth century. My heart was heavy with the memories of elementary school civil defense drills and with growing concern over Vietnam. In the college locker room one day after gym class, I heard in shocked disbelief that John Kennedy had been shot on a Dallas street ten miles away from where I was standing.

A Buddhist monk set himself aflame one day, made the evening news broadcasts, and public opinion began to turn against the Vietnam War. Martin Luther King was killed, and hardened hearts were opened. John Kennedy was assassinated, and his stalled civil rights legislation moved through congress. Jesus was crucified and became the archetype of the age.

Is the archetype of heroic self-destruction a necessary part of the evolution of love? Has the time come in human awareness when the heart can be opened without such violent destruction against its public exponents? A deeper question: Is the warrior still in charge of human destiny, either in his angry, fearful outburst toward the exponents of love or as the warrior for righteousness who is necessarily ready to take on self-destruction in his cause? Can humanity be released from its bondage to the warrior? Can the hero-creative come forth to reign?

When I was in the womb, atomic bombs were exploded over Hiroshima and Nagasaki. Those events have stood over our age like death watching over our shoulder. The atomic age brings to our collective mind the same existential threat that we each feel when face to face with our individual death. Humanity can no longer bear the luxury of living in unconscious bondage to the tyranny of the warrior.

The warrior's sword is a symbol of the transformation for which we long. Can that sword be turned from battle into the sword of truth, discrimination, and insight? Can its metallic strength become the strength of the backbone, giving the ability to stand in full power and submit to the yet higher power of divine love? Has the time come when the warrior's sword needs to be balanced by the softness of his romantic love and his physical strength matched by spiritual discipline?

But the deeper question is, whether without giving up his strength, the warrior can be converted, be tamed with the insights of the hero-transcendent and give birth to the hero-creative, unleashing his strength and authority for healing the world in which he has been a captive of violence.

In my relationship with the archetypal warrior, I find him weary of death, weary of destruction, yet enormously frustrated with the powerful aggressive energies he has cultivated through the centuries. He longs to be well used, to be put to meaningful service, and to breathe lustfully into life. The hero-transcendent, on the other hand, knows much about receptivity, about the release of the self into divine contemplation, into silence, into radiant at-one-ment with God. Yet he is at war with his own passions, with his desire for love and ordinary life. The hero-warrior's constant companion is a flirtation with death. He lives his life in a dance of daring, perhaps hoping to fall victim to the sword, and so to end the awful strife in which he lives and to rest in the victor's sweet reward.

Opposing the warrior, in a severe renunciation of his ways of passion and action, stand the early monastics of the Christian era. These sturdy souls went into the desert regions to fast, to live alone, and to face the beasts within. They sought a transcendent realm beyond the devouring hegemony of martial Rome. They found an interior chaos, for which they proposed the solution of becoming passionless. Their route to transcendent rest involved a renunciation of all earthly pleasure. In their taming of the passions, we find the roots of Western spirituality, which has pitted life in the flesh against the life of the spirit.

The call to work creatively in the world was issued by Yahweh to Abraham, Isaac, Jacob, Joseph, Moses, and many others. With the rise of courtly tradition in the High Middle Ages, a fresh vision of Western male life emerged, bringing together the ancient call of God to heroic service, the quest for transcendence, and the creative spirit. In the traditions of the quest for the Holy Grail, there is a marriage of the warrior and the saint in a new hero-creative. The knight sought to use his skills on behalf of the expressed needs of his community. He learned also to give his heart to a woman. The rich symbols of the Grail quest offer a reconciliation between the life of the warrior enmeshed in flesh and the life of the monastic enraptured with heaven.

The Journey toward Health

Our task is to make a healing journey into the Western male soul, looking for the roots of our inner division between the urges of the flesh and the struggles toward transcendence. Our hope is to discover mythic images and practical means for healing our contemporary struggles. We will trace the development of male consciousness through the last four thousand years, from the era of the Fall to the present age. The Fall marks the separation from the feminine-dominated consciousness of the era of the Great Mother worship. The Fall is the dawning in collective human consciousness of its separation from nature and from its previously accessible gods.

Through several diverse mythologies of the Middle East and the West, this shift in human consciousness can be dated around 2000 B.C.E. It is concurrent with the rise of male-dominated religion. We will begin our journey at that point, examining the origins of the Fall and the implications of the separation of humanity from nature and from its worship of the Great Mother.

We will then address the hero-warrior and the hero-transcendent. We will seek fresh understandings of these two figures. I propose that they both stand in opposition to the older unity with nature. The hero-warrior has systematically sought to subdue nature. The hero-transcendent has sought to transcend nature. Later, when we examine the hero-creative, we will explore the Grail quest as providing the images of the hero-creative, who is capable of reconciling spirit and flesh to make genuinely fresh gifts to earthly life.

The hero theme sets the framework for our journey into the male soul, because it so strongly manifests in the mythology and sacred stories during the rise of the masculine era in the evolution of human consciousness. The hero's journey as told in myth, legend, and scriptures throughout the world reflects the plight of humanity emerging into self-consciousness. Such stories are full of suffering, battles with serpent monsters, descent into the underworld, and ascent to the upperworld. The hero myths give us very graphic images of the collective mind in its struggle to establish an identity separate from nature. The myths of the heroes have a predominantly masculine flavor, for they emerged at the time when humanity turned from the worship of the divine in the form of the Great Mother to the worship of God the Father. This era saw the rise of Judaism, the Greek pantheon with Zeus as ruler, and the emergence of Ra, the sun god, in ancient Egypt. This epoch precedes the Christian era and is its foundation.

The myths of ancient Greece reflect this era strikingly and represent a bridge between the world of the ancient Great Mother and that of God the Father. There are also many themes of Greek mythology that were brought forward into Christianity. For these reasons, we will begin the mythic journey with an analysis of the hero-warrior and hero-transcendent archetypes in Greek mythology.

The story of the slaying of Typhon provides intriguing metaphors for the emerging masculine consciousness. Typhon is the last son of Gaia, Earth, representative of the old feminine consciousness identified with the rhythms and cycles of nature. Zeus, the new masculine consciousness, slays Typhon using two implements: a steel sickle and his lightningbolt. We will explore these two metaphors as representative of the two modes of masculine separation from the enmeshment in nature. The sickle represents the hero-warrior in the ability to forge and use metals in subduing the earth. The lightningbolt represents the hero-transcendent in his quest for enlightenment. Another fascinating theme from Zeus is that he has two sons, Hercules and Dionysus, by liaison with earthly women. In those figures, we again find the polar theme: the hero-warrior in Hercules and the hero-transcendent in Dionysus. The myths of Dionysus provide an important bridge into the themes of Christian spirituality and thus into our present age. Other stories of interaction between brothers will also assist our discoveries, such as the interaction between Romulus and Remus and the tragedy of Cain and Abel.

The seeds of reconciliation between these polar forces are present in the early roots of Hebrew thought and in the image of God as creator calling forth a creative humanity. Jesus stands in the middle of this saga as the figure of supreme moral authority over Western life. In his surrender to God, we find the epitome of the balance needed to Western male aggression; in his resurrection, he summons us to receive authority as cocreators of earth with God. As we bring these issues toward contemporary life, we will work with historic figures such as St. Paul and St. Augustine, as well as with the more contemporary legends of the Holy Grail. Toward the end of this journey, we will also explore themes in writers including Friedrich Nietzsche, Nikos Kazantzakis, and D. H. Lawrence.

I am grateful to the contemporary men who have shared some of their inner life with us in these pages. Whenever I have included my own vision and dream materials, I have clearly identified them as such. I hope, thereby, to share my movement toward resolution on these issues. I have identified my own experiences for another reason as well. I believe that we are entering an era in which men and women will increasingly experience an opening to transpersonal realms, the realms of dreams, visions, and interior journeying. And by identifying my own inner experience I hope to make my small contribution toward encouraging us to communicate with one another about our excursions into these realms. Much health, I believe, for each of us is to be gained by bringing that which has remained hidden and unspoken into common awareness. In addition, by sharing the richness of these interior realms, we may discover some new collective visions that will beckon us toward healthier forms of common life.

My personal saga from originating the ideas for *Healing the Male Soul* to some resolution with these themes has taken ten years, five years devoted to interior understanding and five years to external manifestation. These years have been arduous but necessary years of midlife transition. I have found in this passage of years a fierce and demanding as well as a loving and compassionate God. I have found the warrior within the saint and the saint within the warrior within myself, and everywhere the hero-creative seeking to manifest himself. I hope to stir these same themes in the reader and to further a resolution of these themes so that genuine health and creativity may be brought forth from each of us.

The era of masculine predominance is ending, not only in the workplace, but also in the inner spaces of the heart. A Protestant, steeped in anti-Catholic history, may suddenly find his prayer directed to the Blessed Virgin. Such bewildering turns of the spirit seem to be abounding in our age. In the intrapsychic realms there appears to be a growing emergence of feminine deities in Western consciousness (Neumann 1963; Perera 1981; Whitmont 1982; Woolger 1989). There is also a strong interest among both men and women in moving beyond stereotypic sex roles and self-images (Singer 1977). The world sociopolitical alliances are changing and shifting almost daily on a massive scale.

In light of these current phenomena, when we seem to be witnessing the passing of an era of human history in the unfolding evolution of consciousness, it is critical that we explore the unique qualities of the Western male experience. There are many boons as well as demons in our cultural and mythical heritage. These factors dwell within the male soul and dominate our self-concepts until we bring them to consciousness. In order to illumine this heritage, we will explore some of the dominant themes in the hero's journey of this era. We will look for those values which we need to bring forward with us into the emerging world of our time, in which intercultural communication is taking place and sex roles are changing. What can we learn from the mythology of the masculine era (roughly the last four thousand years of human history)? What do we need to do to facilitate healing within ourselves as men now that the masculine era is coming to an end with the reemergence of the feminine? Are there distinctively masculine ways to heal our inner turmoils?

The questions that we will address revolve around three central themes: power, love, and creativity. The hero-warrior has much to teach us about power, about the ability to overcome hardship through disciplined effort and the cultivation of personal and collective authority. The hero-transcendent has much to teach us about love and about the cultivation of human community through surrender to divine authority and vision. The hero-warrior stands in Western psychology as the model for the development of egoic strength and unique individual identity. The hero-transcendent teaches us to surrender the ego in order to serve the whole of humanity and God. The hero-creative teaches us to honor all aspects of human life, flesh and spirit, as the material we need to confront the challenges of our time. The hero-creative challenges us to attain our stature and to "be as gods" in offering our creative energy for the renewal of planetary life.

At the beginning of Western spiritual history stands God the creator, bringing forth the earth and blessing all forms of creaturely life. Humanity is brought forth in God's "image" (Gen. 1:27). And humanity is given authority over the earth. The authority that humanity is given is the authority of cocreation with God of earthly life. In humanity's efforts to claim the awesome responsibility of this role there have been many difficulties. The atomic and ecological ages awaken us to the danger of such cocreation. Inherent in the authority of creation is the authority of destruction. The masculine principle has unleashed enormous power to humankind. Jesus offers a balance to this unbridled masculine principle in his witness to serve all of humanity and his own surrender in the crucifixion. Earthly life cannot now survive if our acquired masculine power is not balanced by a loving surrender into reverence for all the forms of earthly life.

The hero-warrior and the hero-transcendent challenge us to the awakening of our total beings as the hero-creative, beings of flesh and spirit, body and soul, imagination and reason, power and love. Through such awakening we may begin healing the male soul.

Experiential Questions

The experiential questions at the end of each chapter are provided to assist you in making the material from that chapter relevant to your own life. They are designed as questions for pondering and writing. I encourage you to keep your responses throughout the reading of the book. Some of the questions in later chapters refer to your ponderings on questions from previous chapters.

1. Turn to the model of the hero's journey in Figure 1. As you think of the current phase of your life as a hero's journey, what is the present call to adventure? This call to adventure may be very recent, or it may have occurred a few years ago. You may find that you have different calls to adventure, with different challenges in several arenas of your life: family, primary relationship, career, personal spiritual development, or others. Name each call as clearly as you can. Then look at all of them and find a central call to characterize this phase of your life.

2. Who or what are your current tests? The tests come in the form of internal challenges within our own personality. They also come as external people who challenge us, and they come as external life situations.

3. Who or what are your helpers? One of the gifts of the hero's journey in mythology and sacred scripture is that help is available to us. One of our tasks is to identify and ask for the help we need. What kind of helpers might you ask for that you do not now have?

4. What is the prize of this quest? What are you really seeking? It may be helpful to ask this question in terms of your relationship with God. What quality of relationship with God are you seeking to realize through this quest? What personal characteristics are you manifesting through this quest? What actual tasks are you seeking to achieve for yourself or others?

5. Think back to your late childhood and early adolescence. Often, as the question for this book came from my childhood, we will find that we are living out challenges we posed to ourselves when we were in late childhood or early adolescence. When you look back, do you find any connection between this current quest and issues and questions about life that you posed to yourself at that young age?

6. What threshold struggles have you encountered either in entering into this quest or seeking to return the prize into the world? If you are beginning the quest, what threshold challenges might you anticipate? If you are beginning the return, what struggles with the threshold of return might you anticipate? One of the traps of spirit-

ual growth is to imagine that, because we have changed inwardly, there will be an easy resonance of our inward change into the world. Instead, it may be quite challenging because we now are bringing a new self-understanding into our world.

7. How will you know that you are sharing the prize with the world, how will you know that you are giving the elixir to others? That is to say, how will you measure the success of this venture and be able to say, it is complete?

8. Do you find yourself identifying more with the hero-warrior, the hero-transcendent, or the hero-creative as briefly described in this chapter? What are the positive and negative aspects of each of these in terms of your life experience and self-awareness?

2

♦ ♦ ♦

ORIGINAL SIN RECONSIDERED

> Wherever I turned there was evil upon evil.
> Misery increased, justice departed,
> I cried to my god, but he did not show his countenance;
> I prayed to my goddess, she did not raise her head.
> . . . .
>
> Death is before me today:
>   Like the home that a man longs to see,
>   After years spent as a captive. (Wilber 1981b, 288–89)

These words of terrible inner suffering were written around 1750 B.C.E. by Tabi-utul-Enlil in Babylon. They reflect a new epoch in human history as evidenced in the mythic record. Prior to this time there is no record in literature of existential human suffering. Gods and goddesses play out their roles, humanity performs its functions. But suddenly, the gods fall silent, and humanity perceives itself to be cast out of relationship with the gods in an intimate way and forced to come to terms with life and death. "'There is no trace whatever of such concerns in any literature previous to [these] texts . . .'" (Wilber 1981b, 288).

In *Up From Eden* (1981b), Ken Wilber has correlated mythological motifs with evolutionary history. He correlates the Fall and the universal sense of alienation from the gods with the evolutionary development of the capacity for rational thought and a separate sense of self. In terms of historical evidence from myth and sacred texts, he dates the Fall as an existential crisis occurring around three to four thousand years ago, roughly 1000 to 2000 B.C.E. His thesis is that the primordial Eden did not represent a higher state of consciousness than egoic development, in which we are so painfully aware of contradiction, duality, good and evil, but rather that the

Eden state represents an earlier era of human history, one in which humanity has not yet consciously distinguished itself from nature.

In the mythologies of the era prior to this awakening consciousness, there was a predominance of ritual and worship associated with the fertility of nature. The predominant figure was the feminine goddess. This goddess had a series of male consorts, usually sacrificed after a period of association with the goddess. The Great Mother is a term broadly used to apply to these particular strains of myth and religious practice, in which the fecundity remains with the feminine. There is a high degree of association between this feminine figure and the fecundity of nature. We have an indirect glimpse into these worship forms in the Old Testament descriptions of the worship of Baal among the Canaanites. And we note there the terrible animosity between this older form of religion and the new worship of an interior power, Yahweh, the new God, who will identify himself only as "I am that I am," a force clearly beyond nature, a kind of intelligence that is beyond anything that is in created form.

There is a dark side to the Great Mother, requiring rituals of sacrifice, including human sacrifice. We may say that, in her worship, human consciousness has not yet made the distinction between life and death and undertaken to struggle against death. Humanity has not yet become "Israel," struggling with God and human life and prevailing. If the god or goddess seems to require human sacrifice, then so be it. With Tabi-utul-Enlil's plaintive cry, we hear a new agony of human awareness, a man alone before life and death.

In the Old Testament story of Eden, we find an innocence similar to that of the Great Mother era. In Eden, Adam and Eve are naked, but they do not know it. Sometimes God walks along with them in the garden, sometimes not, but they suffer no feelings of fear when he is absent. They simply tend the garden without personal initiative. There is an instruction not to eat of the tree of the knowledge of good and evil, to stay in blissful ignorance. They seem to be in union with nature and content. But their contentment rests on ignorance. They have not yet fully looked into the jaws of death and into the responsibilities of creating their world. Once they taste of the tree of the knowledge of good and evil, and therefore begin to call some things about life good and others evil, they are irrevocably awakened from their state of Edenic slumber.

That knowledge and that responsibility coupled with the ability to stand apart from nature is the Fall. And it correlates with the ascendency of masculine gods. The most prominent of all these god figures in Western history is named "I am that I am." Yahweh gives us the foremost task of this era of human history, to be able to stand as a unique individual against the forces of nature and the conflicts of cultures, to be able to imitate him and say, "I am."

In *The Origins and History of Consciousness*, Eric Neumann presents one of the first and most comprehensive studies of the evolution of human consciousness, as correlated with the historic patterns of religious and mythic awareness. His view is that the hero myths, the rise of egoic consciousness in humanity, and the shift from the worship of the Great Mother to God the Father are all correlated developments. For him, the tasks of the hero and the tasks of ego development are one and the same. This task is a masculine task, it is the task of active self-consciousness. "The awakening ego experiences its masculinity, i.e., its increasingly active self-consciousness, as good and bad at once. It is thrust out from the maternal matrix, and it finds itself by distinguishing itself from this matrix" (Neumann 1954, 138).

We discover many of these tasks in the stories of the Old Testament, as a people struggles to come to self-consciousness and moral awareness within the milieu of the ancient Middle East. We discover Abraham struggling with the practice of human sacrifice when God asks him to sacrifice his son, Isaac. Human sacrifice was practiced widely in this ancient world (Speiser 1964, 165). Yet Abraham, when directly confronted with this practice, finds instead that he is released from its bondage. What becomes paramount in Abraham's story is not the appeasement of an angry and unpredictable god or goddess of nature, which keeps humanity bound in fear to the processes of death. Instead, Abraham finds that this new God promises to take him toward a future beyond his own generation. If Abraham had sacrificed Isaac, not only would he have lost the beloved son of his old age, he would have lost the forward-tending promise of God that he had heard earlier, a promise that would take generations to fulfill. Thus, in this saga of Western consciousness, we find humanity taking the responsibility of cocreation with God, that relies on a vision transcending even the life of a single generation. We find humanity aiming itself toward a future wholeness, which can only begin when we also take on the task of consciously wrestling with the limitations of each present reality.

This thrust into conscious awareness of life and death and of individual authority is also found in early Greek literature. The gradual development of the term "I" to mean a subjective state of consciousness is illustrated in the stories collected by Homer into the *Iliad* and the *Odyssey* (Jaynes 1976). In the *Iliad*, which records legends predating those of the *Odyssey,* motivating factors are generally bodily parts, the *thymos* (the liver and gross motor agitation) or the *phrenes* (the rapid movement of breathing). The hero acts in the *Iliad* because something in his body is agitated. In the later stories of the *Odyssey,* the terms *noos* (seeing) and *psyche* become much more predominant. The hero acts because he "sees" the situation. There is an emerging inner something beyond various stimuli that is the center of action. Even so, in the *Odyssey, psyche* has not yet taken on full subjectivity; it is simply that which flows out when one dies (ibid., 255–77).

By the sixth century B.C.E., in the writing of Solon, we are at home with people of similar consciousness to our own. *Noos* is Solon's operative concept. *Noos* has taken on all the qualities of subjective awareness, which bring to it the connotations of insight as well as sight. Solon speaks of *noos* as being developed over a period of time and fully intact for a man at age forty-two. And he warns his fellow Athenians that they cannot blame their gods for their misfortunes, but must blame themselves (ibid., 286). Thus, in Greece, the development of modern consciousness, with its shift of responsibility from the voices of the gods to oneself, takes place from 1000 to 600 B.C.E. The period prior to that is characterized by great upheaval both geographically and psychically. The "I am" reflected in Hebrew development is found in the Greek concept of *noos.*

A similar development can be perceived in the patchwork of writings making up the Old Testament. In some cases, like Abraham, the hero figure hears God and immediately acts, without the struggle of self-consciousness. In other writings, like Ecclesiastes, the author ponders the changes of life from a center of existential ego-consciousness within himself. He has become fully subjective, able to judge life from his vantage point of good and evil and say, "Vanity of vanities, all is vanity" (Eccles. 1:2; ibid., 296). In the earliest stories of the Old Testament, the story of creation, of the flood, and of the tower of Babel, these great existential themes are presented. We find humanity there described as "heightened" above the other creatures of the earth "through his knowledge of, and freedom for, good and evil." Yet, "he has difficulties in finding the right balance of his existence, and is overbearingly inclined to reach out toward the divinity of which he is only an image" (Voegelin 1956, 17). In short, we have the struggle of modern existential consciousness. This consciousness has been developed through "the consciousness of death," and "overpowering natural disasters," as well as the discovery of a vast diversity of peoples and cultures (ibid.).

The biblical stories of Adam and Eve's expulsion from a docile existence in Eden and the overpowering flood find a historical correspondence in the dislocations brought by natural disaster throughout the Mediterranean and Mesopotamian regions in the second millennium B.C.E. There is evidence for the eruption of a volcano on the island of Thera, also called Santorini, some sixty miles north of Crete. This event coincided with a massive collapse in the ocean floor. Clouds of volcanic ash hung over the region for days, and a seven-hundred-foot-high tidal wave smashed along the coasts of the Aegean. The date of this event is set by some at 1470 B.C.E. and by others between 1180 and 1170 B.C.E., when Cyprus, the Nile delta, and the coast of Israel all suffered calamity (Jaynes 1976, 212–13). It has also been suggested that this disaster may have led to the sudden disappearance of the Minoan culture of Crete (Eisler 1987). These disasters accelerated an already occurring process of separation of human consciousness from a comfortable relationship with nature. Disasters reigned, with peoples uprooted and with the Assyrian warriors moving out in conquest. The old world order, with its predominant form of worship as the worship of the Great Mother, came to an end in the Mesopotamian and Mediterranian worlds. The two thousand years prior to the birth of Christ and the beginning of the present age were marked by an upheaval of consciousness, giving rise to the emergence of rational thought and resultant egoic consciousness.

After this review of developments in the two thousand years before Christ, Erich Neumann's words describing the concurrent development of ego-consciousness and masculine consciousness reverberate with greater authority: "The awakening ego experiences its masculinity, i.e., its increasingly active self-consciousness, as good and bad at once. It is thrust out from the maternal matrix, and it finds itself by distinguishing itself from this matrix" (1954, 138). Thus the tasks of the present era were set in motion during this period of great dislocation in the Mediterranean and Middle Eastern world. During the masculine era, humanity has been learning to stand on its own and has been learning to take dominion over itself and over nature. The hero-warrior is the archetypal expression of this capacity to take authority and to learn to live with one's individual and collective power. He has been the hero of mythology doing battle with the serpent monster, the remnant of the old unconscious unity with nature, with the feminine, and with the Great Mother. Now that he has reached a point of absolute equality with nature, that is, the ability to destroy life as it is known on the earth, it is necessary to enter into a new relationship with nature and with God, a relationship of cocreation. The hero-transcendent has been guardian of the capacity for direct knowing of the mysterious forces beyond the intellect, yet his way of attaining these mysteries in the West has been couched in a denial of earthly pleasures. The era of the hero-creative is upon us, demanding of each of us as men to be separate from the earth, standing in our own warrior power, while also listening for the call of the divine. In a new creative union with the earth and with woman, the hero-creative blesses earthly life. Let us now turn to some of the mythological themes of the Fall, which set the stage for these developments of Western consciousness.

Rejection of the Great Mother

A predominant theme in Western mythologies is the rejection of the feminine. The Fall marks a turning against the old order of the previous religious structure. It is a rebellion against humanity's identification with nature. The older Great Mother religions found religious meaning in the rhythms of nature, the cycles of planting, cultivating, and reaping. Such seasonal activities were accompanied by festivals, sacrifices, and orgiastic rites, which celebrated humanity's unity with the natural functions of creation. A picture of what is perhaps the zenith of this culture is given by Riane Eisler in her description of the Minoan culture of Crete, with its emphasis on equality of the sexes, play, and natural physicality (Eisler 1987).

What distinguishes both Hebrew and Greek thought from this previous world view is an emergence of central authority in the cosmos, which becomes analogous to the emerging of central authority of the ego within individual consciousness. Humanity no longer looks to a multitude of gods and goddesses, but to the central God, who has authority over all creation. The Hebrews no longer looked to nature for God but beyond nature to the God who is not multiple but "one." "Hear, O Israel, the Lord our God, the Lord is One" (Deut. 6:4; Smith 1991, 274–75).

Although Greek religion maintains its pantheon of gods and goddesses, Greek philosophy moves into the direction of seeking the unifying principle beyond all forms. There is, in fact, a curious parallel in Greek mythology to this focus on a unifing divine order. Zeus becomes supreme ruler of Olympus. Not only on Olympus does he reign, but he also creates the world anew. He exerts authority over all the powers of earth and heaven. His uncontested authority is illustrated in a scene from the *Iliad* (8.17ff), in which Zeus challenges all the Olympians:

> "Then [you] will see how far I am strongest of all the immortals. Come, you gods, make this endeavor, that you all may learn this. Let down out of the sky a cord of gold; lay hold of it all you who are gods and all who are goddesses, yet not even so can you drag down Zeus from the sky to the ground, not Zeus the high lord of counsel, though you try until you grow weary. Yet whenever I might strongly be minded to pull you, I could drag you up, earth and all and sea and all with you, then fetch the golden rope about the horn of Olympos and make it fast, so that all once more should dangle in mid air. So much stronger am I than the gods, and stronger than the mortals." (Eliade 1978, 252)

Here, Zeus establishes his omnipotence and his unifying function. No longer will the pantheon of gods and goddesses, of powers whether mortal or immortal, each go freely on their own way. Instead, they are unified by the supreme ruler. Through this new order of transcendent unity, a golden cord containing the gods and goddesses stretches from earth to the heavens and ultimately to Zeus. This golden thread is reminiscent of Jacob's ladder of ascent. Symbolically, human attention is turned toward the heavenly realms and away from the powers of the earth.

The Greek alienation with nature in pursuit of a new idealized masculine consciousness also takes the unfortunate turn of creating an alienation with woman. In Greek myth, after Prometheus has bestowed the gift of fire on man, Pandora (the gift of woman) is sent by Zeus as a *punishment* to man. Pandora, a name that means "the rich in gifts" and the "all-giving," is also a name of the earth itself (Kerényi 1951, 219). Whereas before, the earth was seen in myth to be a place without evil, sickness, and death, the woman, Pandora, releases these troubles upon humanity (ibid., 218). In Greek myth, we thus have described the essential points made in the Hebrew story of the Fall. The giving of fire, and the ability to manipulate it, is the awakening of rational and moral capability similar to the eating of the tree of the knowledge of good and evil by Adam and Eve in the Garden of Eden. Pandora creates death, disease, and trouble upon the earth. These troubles are certainly not new upon the earth, but we have humanity now awakening to them and beginning to struggle against them.

Earth, the giver of gifts, has become the source of suffering. And humanity has put enmity between itself and suffering. Suffering now becomes the serpent monster against which man heroically struggles. Man becomes conquerer and subduer of the earth. It is intriguing that it is Zeus, the new male god, who sets this enmity in motion. The male god creates enmity with the earth. Several shifts in human awareness occurred at the same time: the triumph of male dieties, the emergence of rational thought, and the development of an independent center of self-consciousness that we ordinarily call the ego. The result of these developments was a repudiation of the instinctual world of the Great Mother. "Reason and instinct are at war" in the West (Wilber 1981b, 194). The Fall is the beginning of cultural discourse. Unfortunately, the emerging thought world rebelled not only against the darkness of the old Earth Mother, with her rituals of sacrifice and communal sexuality. Male-dominated ego-consciousness rebelled against woman. With the development of rational thought and the concurrent suppression of the body's instinctual drives in the service of ideals, the ascending male-dominated cultures also suppressed women.

While Hebrew culture gave much prominence to women, many of these same attitudes can be seen. The lineage of Abraham's promise is passed through the males of the society. Furthermore, it is passed through the ritual of circumcision on the men of the society. This rite, while practiced in different regions of the ancient world, came to be identified as the pivotal sign of faithfulness to the Hebrew God during the period of the Babylonian captivity in the sixth century B.C.E. In that culture, where circumcision was not practiced, it became the distinguishing mark of this small exiled people (von Rad 1962, 83). Furthermore, Babylonian society practiced temple prostitution. Hebrew men were thus physically naked and set apart to worship in an inward way.

Throughout the Old Testament, there are glimpses of the struggle through the centuries for this new consciousness to distinguish itself from the prevailing Great Mother forms of religion. In Deuteronomy, men and women are explicitly prohibited from being temple prostitutes (23:17). In 2 Kings, Josiah takes all the forms of Baal and Asherah out of the temple and abolishes male temple prostitution. Herodotus confirms the use of temple prostitution in Babylon in a writing from the fifth centery B.C.E. (Saggs 1962, 350–51).

Thus it is not incorrect to speak of a major shift of consciousness during this era, which we see both in the development of Hebrew moral and theological reflection and in Greek philosophy and drama. We witness the birth of existential consciousness in a dramatic disruption from nature. This disruption is witnessed in the radical change in religious practice, which shifted from a bodily centered use of sexuality in ritual and from a sacrificial system of propitiating and placating the capricious gods and goddesses of nature, to the worship of an unnamed One, whose primary concern was the deliverance of downtrodden peoples from captivity of other powers.

We can also witness the break with nature and with the Great Mother in the use of symbols. Accompanying the emergence of humanity into self-consciousness in Greek mythology, the Typhon appears. This figure (Figure 4) has a human torso and head but two serpent tails. He is identified as the youngest son of Gaia or Earth (Kerényi 1951, 26). In descriptions of him, he sounds much like a volcano.

> Hissing and bellowing, he flung fiery stones at Heaven, and from his mouth spurted flames instead of spittle. It was still uncertain whether or no Typhoeus would gain mastery over gods and men. But Zeus struck him from afar with lightning, and at close range with the steel sickle, and pursued him to Mount Kasion. (ibid., 26–27)

The Typhon is clearly one of the destructive powers of the earth, perhaps the volcanic mountain, spewing forth stones and fire, and threatening human existence. Or to put these themes another way, the earth's destructive power has now come fully into humanity's consciousness. The new god, Zeus, with the human parallel in the

Fig. 4. Reproduced by permission of the publisher from Ken Wilber, *Up From Eden: A Transpersonal View of Human Evolution* (Garden City, N.Y.: Anchor Press/Doubleday, 1981), p. 42.

emergence of the rational mind, strikes down the last child of earth with his lightning mind and in hand-to-hand combat. The heroic battle with the serpent monster and with the whims of nature has begun.

The history of the serpent is also indicative of a radical shift of consciousness and indicative of the West's alienation from nature, in its alienation from the Great Mother. The serpent has a noble history. It appeared within the rituals of the Great Mother, often seen by mythologists as a symbol for wholeness, the union of infant with mother in undifferentiated oneness. The serpent biting its tail (the uroborus) conveys this image of wholeness. In Crete, the priestess is often depicted as holding the serpents (Figure 5). There we witness the alliance of the Great Mother with the earthly powers. In the healing temples of Asklepios, serpents played a prominent part. The serpent is also a part of Moses' story. Nevertheless, in the Western motif of the Fall the serpent plays the predominant role in awakening Adam and Eve to their unconscious condition. Could it in fact be that by becoming aware of the good and evil aspects of nature, for which the serpent is the symbol, Adam and Eve are awakening to moral reasoning and to rational capability? In later myth, the serpent finally becomes the beast, the symbol of evil, against which the heroes and saints will do battle.

Fig. 5. Snake Goddess, Knossos. Faience, 13½" high, c. 1600 B.C.E. Archeological Museum, Herakleion.

[7]And there was war in Heaven: Michael and his angels fought against the dragon; and the dragon fought and his angels,
[8]And prevailed not; neither was their place found anymore in heaven.
[9]And the great dragon was cast out, that old serpent, called the Devil, and Satan, which deceiveth the whole world: he was cast out into the earth, and his angels were cast out with him.
(Rev. 12:7–9; Quispel 1979, 78)

It is not only in Judeo-Christian symbology that the serpent suffers, however. In Greek mythology, we find the evil potential of the serpent in Medusa, whose countenance ringed with writhing serpents causes instant death to anyone who looks upon it. Perseus, one of the great heroes of emerging consciousness, must slay Medusa (Hamilton 1969, 141–48). In another intriguing use of serpent power for the infliction of death, Athene sends serpents to punish Laocoön and his sons. Laocoön was the priest of Troy who tried to warn the Trojans against allowing the Greek horse within their walls. Because Laocoön has been a voice of reason, seeking to rouse the Trojans against a blind acceptance of the "divine" horse, he is punished by twin serpents swimming through the sea and crushing him and his two sons (ibid., 198).

In Western mythology, Hebrew as well as Greek, the evil nature of the serpent becomes differentiated from its healing power. In this symbolic shift from the serpent as possessing the properties of healing to its association with death, we experience a symbolic differentiation of the good and evil aspects of nature and of the Great Mother. No longer is she simply *all* to an unconscious humanity, slumbering within the confines of nature, yet oblivious to death. We begin to know nature as both benevolent and destructive. In the new order of masculine gods, nature and the Great Mother worship associated with nature come to be identified with evil.

Serpent energy from this time forward has a dual role in the mythology of the West. In the upright intertwined caduceus of Asklepios, the twin serpents stand for health and healing. But they can also be used for destruction when Athene sends the twin serpents to kill Laocoön and his sons. Hera also sends twin serpents to kill the infant Hercules. Instead, Hercules strangles the snakes, and we have no doubt that his warrior life is demonstrated in that encounter! From then on Hercules is the new masculinity asserting its authority over the earth and any earthbound monsters that must be subdued.

The power of nature is now understood to be capable of destruction as well as healing. The discriminating rational-egoic mind makes this discovery, and the awesome responsibility of being one's own authority in a world of good and evil emerges. Earth and heaven are set apart, with earth becoming identified as a vicious evil to be subdued, and with heaven becoming identified with emerging rationalism. This dualistic mind of Western consciousness comes to flower in the age of rationalism with the rise of science in the seventeenth and eighteenth centuries C.E., but at a great price. Along with the triumph of rationalism came the European catastrophe of the punishment of so-called witches who practiced an earthly, feminine, intuitive knowledge and who were ferreted out as heretics and burned (Achterberg 1990). Our European heritage has continued this dualistic mode of thinking in its pogroms and its trials in the quest for religious purity. An intriguing symbolic representation of the triumph of reason is the eighteenth-century cathedral figure of St. George slaying the dragon. This figure shows great pride in the human power to overcome the "beast" of the earth (Figure 6).

However, our rationalism became so alienated from deeper self and from the world of nature that even the psyche became split. It was left for modern psychology to rediscover the unconscious and the deeper self in the twentieth century. The remnant of this initial split with nature and with the Great Mother is the existential dread we each know in the face of death and the fragility of earthly existence. Our health begins in accepting this reality. The farther we push this old serpent away from us, the more profoundly alienated we become from our deeper selves, our bodies, our emotions, and our loved ones. Let us turn our attention to the legacy of this deep divide in human existence.

Pandora's Destructive Power

The fight with nature is with us still, in spite of the enormous strides of our medical science in health and our technological sophistication in providing comforts for life. Underlying our collective and individual lives is still the struggle with death and the struggle to live creatively with the threat of death daily to our existence. In a world where a new and deadly virus such as HIV can surprise us and threaten wholesale death, it is difficult not to be overly anxious or despairing.

This potential for nature to turn her destructive capacity upon us is nowhere more evident than in the fragility of fetal life. Every parent knows the anxiety accompanying pregnancy and the concerns over birth defects and a safe delivery. In those moments we are in the grip of nature's capacity as life-giver and destroyer. Stanislav Grof (1975), in his extensive work with the recovery of memory around the womb and birthing experience, has shown that in the

Fig. 6. Egid Quirin Asam, St. George. Polychromed and guilded stucco, 1721. Weltenberg, Benedictine Church.

womb we are in the process of being created and simultaneously exposed to moments of absolute life-threat. We each bear within our unconscious memory this experience of threat to our existence. Where that threat has been severe, it may be the root of later difficulties in trusting life enough to live with creative risk and joy.

This type of encounter with the death dimension of our existence can underlay our psychological struggles in profound ways. In order to show how very deep this encounter with death can be, the following experience of a man under hypnosis is related. In it his experience with life-threat during the process of birth is brought to conscious memory. At the time of the hypnosis session in which he recovered this memory, Jim was thirty-five years old and working as a college administrator. He has had a problem with stuttering since the age of seven. Previously, he had recovered the memory of a series of very painful dental procedures which he had endured at the age of the onset of the stuttering. However, he felt there were deeper issues involved as well. He entered the hypnosis session to discover the earlier events contributing to the stuttering. Finger signals were utilized to indicate yes and no responses to questions the therapist asked.

In response to questions asking when the speech problem was set in motion, the finger signals indicated that the experience was before the age of four and that it was known. Initially the unconscious mind felt that the conscious mind was not ready to receive the memory. So the memory was reviewed unconsciously a few times.

On the second or third times, I had some faint physical sensations, twitching in my arms. On the third time, I had a faint, shadowy scene, a feeling of suffocation. Again the conscious mind was not ready. On the next review I saw a pillow or something. Right after that my body erupted with crying, sobbing, very deep upset. I got a picture that when I was very young, one and a half or something like that, when I was crying and making a lot of noise, my mother got upset with me and put a pillow over me to try to suffocate me to make me shut up. This evoked all sorts of sadness. It seemed like my father was there and very mousey.

Then I got all of this coughing and gagging and mucous in my throat, and I flipped back to a scene of birth. The secondary part was the mucous. The primary part—there were two parts—one, that my mother didn't plan me and didn't really want me. She had wanted to go back to school and this [birth] really screwed that up. Not only was there all this mucous, but I did have the cord wrapped around my neck. It was like her body had somehow wrapped the cord around my neck to get me that way, and if not that way then through all this mucous in my lungs. An incredible amount of sadness.

They were all suffocation images. And what I decided was that to survive, I would have to be very quiet, keep to myself, and essentially not cause any hassle and be very, very good. There was a point at which she told me either verbally or psychically, "Don't you ever say a word about this to anybody." During this I had gone into two re-birthing cycles, the first with tetany and my arms folding up; the second with the birth, with lots of tingling. Then there was another shift, a sense of, "As long as we are here, we might as well go on." Another wave of sadness, "They're not really my family." Which explained why I never really felt real bonded with them. It [the inner voice] went on to say, neither my mother nor I really had a choice, that I had a lot of love I needed to give to the world and I was absolutely needed here. It explained why at the soul level, the family I had wasn't really mine, and that I did feel more at home with other families.

He [therapist] asked if there was anything else I needed, and I said, "Yes. that I have a right to be here." During this, another energy cycle began, waves through my body, except constriction in chest where I was told not to tell anybody. I got the thought to affirm, "I am life." The energy rose up my spine and blew out the third eye, into a cosmic experience where I experienced being life, with a joy for being alive and that I had survived. (At one point I had experienced all the hatred and rage at her, and the therpist affirmed that it was absolutely right to feel these things.) I felt very grateful to him. I looked at the clock and realized all this had taken only an hour. Since the session, I still stutter, but my speech has been better.

In this case, Jim chose to suppress his rage in the service of survival in his family structure, as well as in response to his deeper soul-level commitment to bring love into the world. He reported experiences of asthma as a child, in one case feeling as though he almost died. He responded to this life-threatening situation by preserving life in a positive manner. His rage at his mother disguises his rage at nature, at the fact that coming to birth can be such a threatening experience. His response to this life-threat took on the form of the hero-transcendent, until such time as his egoic structure was strong enough to handle the full force of his rage.

In an interview six months after this session, Jim reported that his stuttering was diminished by about one-quarter. Initially he had experienced a great deal of rage toward his mother. Now that rage has lessened. His relationship to her has come back into balance. He wonders now whether the hypnosis experience portrayed actual events or merely his projections. However, during the session itself, the events seemed very real. He is inclined to believe that he reexperienced actual events. His experience of birthing, with the cord wrapped around his neck, graphically illustrates the threat that nature is able to pose to us all. Nature brings death to all her children.

The fragility of life impacts us especially in times of direct contact with birth and death. In the first two years of my sons' life as infants, I found myself extremely anxious, profoundly aware of not only the fragility of their lives but the fragility of my life and my wife Ruth's life. Without us, that is, were either of us to be killed, their lives would be radically altered. I came to realize that every day in every absence from them, or every absence of Ruth from them, I was truly frightened of the prospect of death intervening. It is an awesome fact of our existence that death is constantly with us. Fortunately or unfortunately, we usually mask this awareness from ourselves and go about our lives as if it is not true. In those eras of our lives, particularly those extended eras such as the infancy of our children or a lengthy process of dying of our parents or others dear to us, we directly confront this fact.

For this reason, the author of one of the great texts of Western spirituality, *The Cloud of Unknowing* (Johnston 1973), written in the fourteenth century C.E., speaks of the sorrow of the fact of human existence.

> Every man has plenty of cause for sorrow but he alone understands the deep universal reason for sorrow who experiences *that he is.* Every other motive pales beside this one. He alone feels authentic sorrow who realizes not only *what he is but that he is. . . .* In a word, he feels the burden of himself so tragically that he no longer cares about himself if only he can love God. . . . Everyone must sooner or later realize in some manner both this sorrow and this longing to be freed. (ibid., 103–4)

This sorrow that we are, this sorrow that we are human beings inevitably caught in the struggle for meaning, inevitably thrust into life while simultaneously aware of death, is the awareness to which humanity awakened two to four thousand years ago.

Original Sin and Male Consciousness

The Fall is the dawning of self-conscious awareness for humanity of the fragility of life. In the Garden of Eden, Adam and Eve eat of the tree of knowledge and become aware of themselves as fragile creatures of nature. Thus the Fall is a fall into consciousness, into awareness of human fragility, isolation, and self-consciousness regarding death (Wilber 1981b, 297–98). As creatures we are separated from God, cast into a wilderness existence to come to our own inner strength, to face the trials of life, to learn to love and create, and to die. The great religions set in motion during the masculine era, Buddhism, Judaism, Christianity, Islam, have each in their own way sought to provide a pathway to give comfort and purpose to human beings cast into the awareness of life's suffering, pain, and death. In Christianity, this Fall is called *original sin*, because it is understood as the most basic or original split within the human being, the split between the individual, God, and nature. From this fundamental split, all evil that individuals inflict on others arises. Christianity posits that until we understand the basic hunger for God, we will seek to ameliorate our fear of nonexistence with a grasping after momentary security and pleasure that is very apt to be amoral at best and overtly abusive of others at worst. The question of Western spiritual life rises plaintively: "Who shall deliver us from the bonds of sin and death?"

The rites of the worship of the Great Mother demonstrate a profound fear of death, although that fear remained unconscious. The sacrificial rites themselves ameliorated the existential dread that in the Fall must be faced head on within each individual. It is the dawning awareness of death and the accompanying realization of the horrors of sacrificial rites that bring the existential moment of the Fall into reality. In the worship of the Great Mother, sacrificial rites returned to the earth her human or animal sons and daughters.

In the ceremonial rites of sacrifice, it is clear that the Great Mother still holds power over the individual. She will return to her that which belongs to her. With the dawning awareness of death and individuality, humanity experiences the Fall and a sense of existential aloneness. But for the first time humanity can entertain the possibility of genuine communion with God beyond the gods, the

Unifier of all life forces. Humanity can become cocreator of human society with this unifying God. The emerging masculine principle, demonstrated in Yahweh, negates humanity's comfortable slumber within the Great Mother and demands an assumption of moral responsibility.

> I hate, I spurn your pilgrim-feasts; I will not accept them, nor look on the buffaloes of your shared-offerings. Spare me the sound of your songs; I cannot endure the music of your lutes. Let justice roll on like a river and righteousness like an ever-flowing stream.
> (Amos 5:21–24, NEB)

These words are spoken directly against one of the Great Mother religions, the religion of the Canaanites. They represent a dominant theme of Hebrew and Western culture, the taking of responsibility for the quality of earthly life. As a collective unit, humanity must now become responsible for itself and assume the powers of life and death that nature possesses. Humanity enters the struggle to become "I am that I am."

A number of scholars, in studying the record of myth, have correlated the evolutionary development of human consciousness with the development of consciousness within the individual. According to this view, individual psychological development can be correlated with the collective development of humanity as evidenced in myth (Neumann 1954; Campbell 1969; Jaynes 1976; Wilber 1981b). According to this perspective, the Fall in mythic story represents the dawning of individual subjectivity and rational capability, which becomes well developed in children in our era around age six to seven. For boys, this means that we have a rather complex beginning. We have first of all been fully identified with the mother and with the feminine, within the womb and in early infancy. Then that union is disrupted with the dawning of awareness on the part of the infant that sometimes the mother does not immediately respond to its every need. The Great Mother is perceived as destructive as well as benevolent. The young child begins to say "No" to establish its separate identity. Meanwhile, the father represents a threat to this dyad, and the young lad enters into both imitation of and a sense of competition with the father. Therefore, from a mythic standpoint, the father also becomes the good father and the devouring father. With this background in early childhood, the young hero begins to set forth to create his unique identity in the world and in his family, to slay the monsters of death and suffering, to win the love of woman, and for the fortunate ones, to reconcile with mother and father, with nature and with God (Campbell 1968a, 61–77). This pattern of heroic interaction with the world is mirrored in the masculinely oriented myths and sacred stories of this era. It is prevalent and seemingly indomitable, as the stories return in the new guises of Star Wars, Superman, and the animated characters that light up the eyes of children every Saturday morning in televised cartoons.

The legacy of the masculine era of human consciousness is this pattern of self-development, in which the child separates from the mother and father and from nature, in order to establish his or her unique selfhood. From this vantage point we are charged with "taking dominion over the earth" and making our unique contribution to humanity. This legacy has given us precious gifts of individual creativity and is at the heart of the democratic principle of political structure, with its unwavering affirmation of the potential of the individual. The legacy of this pattern is also one of gross cruelty to individuals and to nature, as individuals and our human species itself have proven too domineering in their assertion of themselves. We know only too well both the pain and joy of this quest for unique human identity apart from God, mother, father, and nature. Let us turn now to explore some of the essential characteristics of this development and possible solutions to its tragedies, as evidenced in mythic image.

Male consciousness responded to the existential crisis of the knowledge that life is constantly threatened by death through two basic modes modeled in Zeus's destruction of the Typhon: through the lightningbolt or through the steel sickle. I suggest that these metaphors represent the two basic styles of male response to separation from the Great Mother, a spiritual quest symbolized by the lightningbolt, and the physical conquest of the earth symbolized by the steel sickle. The same dynamics are present in the two sons attributed to the union of Zeus with human women: Dionysus and Hercules.

Hercules, the archetypal hero-warrior, represents the attempt on the part of male consciousness to conquer and subdue nature. Dionysus, the archetype of ecstatic spirituality, represents the attempt to transcend nature, as the hero-transcendent. In the succeeding chapters, I will work with these two themes as descriptive of the two primary modes of male consciousness that have dominated Western history in its early development. The hero-creative, as a reconciling force between these polar themes, is present throughout this history, but Western culture has tended to be obsessed with an either/ or dualism in its thinking. This dualism is illustrated by the myths of the twins or brothers, Romulus and Remus and Cain and Abel. We will explore Romulus and Remus later in this chapter. The story of Cain and Abel will set the stage for the discussion of the hero-warrior in chapter 3. These polar themes have been so dominant that only now do we begin to experience any movement beyond this pattern for any substantial number of men. Thus, while men have had the capacity to transcend dualisms and to be true servants of earth and God, true servants of self and other, our dominant historical patterns have not yet brought forth the potential of the hero-creative. We only now begin to see him manifesting as a potentially dominant pattern culturally. Thus we must begin our understanding of the male history of consciousness with an understanding of the conflict between the hero-warrior and the hero-transcendent. The remainder of this chapter will set the groundwork for this discussion.

Both the hero-warrior and the hero-transcendent arise out of the common victory of an emerging masculine predominance over the old feminine earth. They represent the victory of the cultures founded on metallurgy.

> "Smiths and shamans are from the same nest," declares a Yakut proverb cited by Eliade. The allegedly indestructible body of the shaman who can walk on fire is analogous to the quality of a metal brought forth through the operation of fire. And the power of the smith at his fiery forge to produce such immortal "thunderbolt" matter from the crude rock of the earth is a miracle analogous to that of spiritual (viz. Mithraic or Buddhist) initiation, whereby the individual learns to identify himself with his own immortal part. (Campbell 1964, 292)

We recall that it is Prometheus's gift of fire to the humans that sets in motion the Fall into consciousness for human beings in Greek mythology.

In his conquest of Gaul, Julius Caesar recorded the clearly differentiated roles of the knights and the druid priests within that old European culture. The warriors and the priests were the only classes of persons who were given dignity. The druid priests performed public sacrifices and rituals of worship, and instructed the youth. They decided disputes of both civil and criminal nature. They

charted the stars and taught that souls do not die. They were exempt
from military service and from taxation. The other class of distinguished men was that of knights, who were engaged in battle generally each year, either making attacks or responding to them. The
knights were differentiated according to their wealth and the number of liegemen and dependents that each had about him (Campbell
1964, 293–96). Thus, in the culture of Gaul, as well as Greece, the
affinity for the division of powers between the hero-warrior and the
hero-transcendent is well documented.

We have spoken of the separation of masculine consciousness from
the Great Mother as demonstrated in the history of this era. There
is another powerful theme for men in the mythic record, which
speaks of the relationship between fathers and sons. The succession
of power from father to son is an issue of enormous significance,
even in our present time, when life-expectancy is growing and the
period of time between entering mature adulthood and the assumption of significant levels of authority in the workplace seems to be
increasing. We must explore not only the enmity between the masculine and the old feminine, but also the enmity and reconciliation
between forms of masculine service and between fathers and sons.

The primary way in which Christianity has described the re-
deeming work of Christ is as a reconciliation of human beings with
God the Father. The motif of reconciliation with the father is one
of the four major themes cited by Joseph Campbell in his description
of the hero's journey. This theme is common in both the sagas of
the hero-warrior and the hero-transcendent. Will the father relin-
quish his power and authority to the son or must the son wrest it
from the father? In examining the many records of myth, Joseph
Campbell offers the following summary of the relationship between
father and son:

> In the end, the hero, now a youth returning to his proper home,
> either overthrows the father and sets himself in his place (Oedipus,
> Perseus, Christ's New Testament supplanting the Old), or becomes
> reconciled with the father and completes the father's work (the New
> Testament as fulfillment of the Old). (1981, 44)

In Greek mythology, Kronos or Saturn is the father of Zeus. Until
the birth of Zeus, Kronos has devoured all his children. He is a giant
figure and devours his children to avoid being overthrown by them.
Our word *chronology* derives from his name. He is the passing of

time, who in due course devours the children of time. Here is the negative aspect of the father. The role of Saturn in astrology is that of the structuring and ordering of the earthly realm of time. It represents "collective law" (Hand 1981, 69). Thus Kronos or Saturn has come to represent in our present time the often overpowering structures of law and tradition. The positive benefit of this Kronos principle is that of providing structure for developing youth. The negative aspect is that it can literally devour the energy of youth and destroy a society by denying the renewing power of the new energy that the youthful heroes bring to it. In its most demanding aspect, Kronos is the power and authority of an older generation of men to send its youth to war.

While Zeus overcomes Kronos, he does not slay him. Instead, after Zeus's sovereignty has been assured, Kronos is freed from his place of imprisonment in the earth and established as ruler of the kingdom of gold, which becomes the place of reward for noble heroes, who, instead of dying, live the life of primordial paradise (Eliade 1978, 253).

Zeus's victory represents the coming hegemony of rational authority in human endeavors. Zeus represents for the masculine psyche the dominance of rational thought and concern for spiritual ideals over unconscious slumber in natural life, in which we are blindly bound to the devouring Kronos. In Greek mythology, Zeus establishes himself as the unifying principle to all life, similar to the unifying sense of the ego in the psyche. We find in Zeus a parallel to Yahweh as the "one" God, the unifier of the powers of the universe. Zeus seems to give greater authority to the way of the hero-transcendent, yet in Greek mythology, the hero-warriors also have their reward, life with Kronos in the land of gold.

Shall we seek the earthly kingdom ruled over by the warriors and the quest for gold or the heavenly kingdom ruled over by the druids and other priests in their quest for eternal life? Or shall we seek both, as the hero-creative?

A general answer to that question given by Jesus for Western culture is: "No servant can be the slave of two masters; for either he will hate the first and love the second, or he will be devoted to the first and think nothing of the second. You cannot serve God and Money" (Matt. 6:24, NEB). This dualistic view of reality has predominated during the masculine era. Serve God or serve the world. Be a warrior or a priest. In Western history, this polarity has been highly delineated, and often perceived as a contest beween the two modes of service to the father: service to the temporal father in the upbuilding of cities and nations, and service to the Heavenly Father in the upbuilding of the human heart to increase its capacity for compassion.

A doctrine of the two worlds, or the two kingdoms, hovers over Western thought. It is present in the Essene writings at the time of Christ. The thought is reminiscent of the book of Revelation. In both writings a cosmic war is being waged between the Sons of Light and the Sons of Darkness. In both, the Sons of Darkness are identified as those who give primary allegiance to the temporal order. The Sons of Light are those seeking alliance with the Eternal Father. From the perspective of the servants of God the Father, anyone serving lesser authorities is doomed (Campbell 1964, 282–86).

The doctrine of the two kingdoms, the kingdom of earth and the kingdom of God, comes to fulfillment in the writing of Augustine (1950), in the fifth century C.E. He used the terms *civitas Dei*, the city of God, and *civitas terrena*, the earthly city, to describe these two realities. Christ had set these two authorities in reciprocal relationship: "pay Caesar what is due to Caesar, and pay God what is due to God" (Luke 20:25, NEB). The appropriate balance between these two claims has been a constant struggle of Western life. In *The Making of the Modern Mind*, John Randall comments upon medieval life:

> The Middle Ages, as we have already seen, knew two societies, the *civitas Dei* and the *civitas terrena*, the City of God and the Earthly City. Faithful Christians dwelt in both. Just where the boundaries lay, the Middle Ages, for all their searching and their struggles back and forth, were never able to decide; the powers of the two cities were in eternal conflict in the soul of every man. But for ordinary purposes the distinction was clear enough; the City of God was the Church, and wielded the sword of the spirit, the Earthly City was lay society, and exercised the secular sword. In the thirteenth century the spiritual power, under an Innocent III, was unquestionably supreme, then the economic growth of the nations proved too much for it, and, shattered and riven, it has since been largely at the beck and call of temporal monarchs. (1940, 61)

Although the hero-transcendent path often damned the way of the hero-warriors, seeking dominion in earthly matters, it would appear in our time that the cultural norm is closer to the quest for reward in Kronos's land of gold than it is for the unfailing eternal presence of God. Kronos's land of gold looks deceptively like Palm Springs or Miami or the countless other retirement communities we have built to reward ourselves at the end of life with earthly rewards. It has been the fate of Western consciousness to raise the *civitas terrena* above the *civitas Dei*. Those temporal values, once identified with the rule of the earthly city, the province of the hero-warrior, once held in check by the moral authority of the church, have gained ascendency. Bishop Bossuet, in his *Discourse on Universal History,* written at the end of the seventeenth century, comments on the two cities:

> All history was henceforth essentially nothing but the conflict between these two cities; two moralities, one natural, the other supernatural; two philosophies, the one rational, the other revealed; two beauties, the one corporeal, the other spiritual; two glories, the one temporal, the other eternal; two institutions, one the world, the other the Church. These, whatever their momentary alliances or compromises, were radically opposed and fundamentally alien to one another. (Randall 1940, 19–20)

In the final "harvest," Bishop Bossuet dooms the children of nature to "everlasting torments with the devil whom they served" (ibid.). Such doom for the inhabitants of the *civitas terrena* is very far removed from the reward they receive in Greek mythology in Kronos's land of gold.

In the passage of Western history these two visions have vied with each other for prominence. While the vision of the hero-transcendent has been brought to prominence through the Church of Rome, we must also remember that the city of Rome predated Christianity by some seven centuries. The city of Rome was itself founded on warrior principles. The story of its founding is contained in the myth of Romulus and Remus. In the story, as related by Plutarch, they were twins born to the virgin daughter of Amulius, in the royal line of Aeneas. Shortly after her father forced her to take the vows of a Vestal Virgin, she was found to be pregnant. If her cousin had not pleaded for her life, she would have been buried alive in disgrace (Campbell 1964, 313).

When Romulus and Remus were born, they were of uncommon beauty and great size. In alarm, Amulius sent them to a servant to be killed. But the servant put them in a little boat and set it on a river. It came to rest by a wild fig tree. A she-wolf found them and nursed them. A woodpecker brought them food. Plutarch says these two animals were sacred to Mars, and therefore they confirm the girl's story that the father of the children was Mars. Others claimed that her father, disguised in armor as Mars, had come to her and was the father of the children (ibid., 313–14). Figure 7 is the well-known statue of the twins nursing at the she-wolf. It aptly depicts the infancy of masculine consciousness, seeking to differentiate itself from nature and from the Great Mother, depicted as the wolf, while yet actually dependent upon nature. The emblem of the she-wolf nursing the infant twins is an apt metaphor for the new masculine consciousness. The two twins represent the dualistic thinking of the rational mind. Their infancy represents the infant nature of this new way of being. They depend upon the old alliance with nature, but that alliance becomes increasingly unconscious. Henceforth, the arena of human activity will lie not in interaction with nature but with the interaction of men, in their dual modes of service to the father and in their conflict with each other. And the father of the founders of Rome is Mars, the god of war, or a child-abusing father disguised as Mars.

Some stories indicate that the twins were given special attention by their uncle, King Numitor, the brother of Amulius. They were found by Amulius's swineherd and brought up through the king's assistance to go to school and to be well trained in hunting, taking care of the oppressed, and guarding their homeland from thieves. They have become archetypal heroes. In one story, Remus is kidnaped, and his brother attacks the city where he is being held, slays the tyrant king, and saves his brother. After this episode, they bid their mother farewell and set off to found a new city (ibid., 314).

So far, so good. Romulus and Remus are typical hero figures. Romulus rescues his brother from the tyrant, killing him. They represent the new hegemony that sons establish in combat with their fathers, as they set off to found a new city. Very soon, however, trouble arises. They quarrel over the site where the city should stand. They decide to settle their dispute by divination. "But when Remus saw six vultures and Romulus claimed twelve, they came to blows and Remus was slain" (ibid.).

These sons of Mars fail as sons of the transcendent. Their religious intuitions are weaker than their martial art. War, henceforth, is the

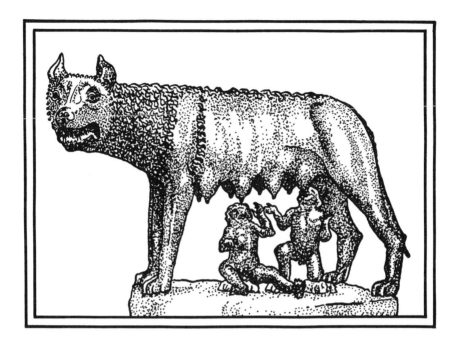

Fig. 7. She Wolf, Bronze, height 33½″, c. 500 B.C.E. Capitoline Museums, Rome.

trademark of Rome. "A quarrel arose," and was settled by the death of one of the disputants. The divination failed to produce mutually agreed upon results, and one of the participants was slain. In this remarkable outcome, we perhaps foresee the tremendous power of the warrior archetype in Western history.

Rome is founded on warrior principles. Romulus procures women for the new city through the famous rape of the Sabines. Rome proceeds to expand its hegemony through war. After Romulus's death or, some said, disappearance, there is a remarkable reappearance very similar in character to Jesus' postdeath appearance to his disciples. He appears to Julius Proculus, who then came before the forum and testified to his appearance under oath. According to Julius Proculus's testimony, Romulus spoke this blessing to Rome:

> "It pleased the gods, O Proculus, that we, who came from them, should remain so long a time amongst men as we did; and having built a city to be the greatest in the world for empire and glory, would again return to heaven. But farewell; and tell the Romans, that, by the exercise of temperance and fortitude, they shall attain the height

of human power; we will be to you the propitious god Quirinus."
(ibid., 316–17)

This appearance of Romulus is strikingly similar to the appearance
of Jesus to his distraught disciples on the road to Emmaus. In that
appearance, recorded in the twenty-fourth chapter of Luke, the resurrected Christ "interpreted to them in all the scriptures the things
concerning himself. . . . When he was at table with them, he took
the bread and blessed and broke it, and gave it to them. And their
eyes were opened, and they recognized him; and he vanished out
of their sight."

In these two postdeath appearances, we have the spirit of the
hero-warrior and the spirit of the hero-transcendent establishing
their respective kingdoms upon the earth. Rome will be the
kingdom of *power.* Christ's kingdom will be the kingdom of *love.*
Romulus's legacy will be hegemonies of earthly empires. Christ's
will be the search for a new form of divination that might bring
accord between people in dispute. Romulus's tool is the sword;
Christ's tool is prayer. Romulus is the son of the Father taking up
the tool of the steel sickle; Christ is the son of the Father taking up
the tool of the lightningbolt.

We find that two of the great themes of male psychology emerge
from this ancient era: leaving the Great Mother and making peace
with the Father through contests with men in the workplace and in
life. These two great themes are, of course, related to our personal
tasks of leaving home, of separating from our mothers and fathers
and of accepting the role set for Adam, to become a wanderer on
the earth. The contest to find the strength of our own resources to
dwell as individual men has begun. The twin quests, the quest for
power and the quest for love, the quest for earthly hegemony and
the quest for heavenly wisdom, emerge as the great challenges of
this era, when humanity is thrust out of its childhood into the quest
for its own adult authority.

In the following chapters, I will discuss the two major forms in which
this masculine life has manifested under the themes of the hero-warrior and the hero-transcendent, each establishing in its own way the
masculine authority over the earth. I will examine the psychological
implications for contemporary men of this historic Western split between the quest for power and the quest for love. I will suggest that
Bishop Bossuet's conclusion, that "the two cities, always opposite in

essence, would thus be finally divided in existence" (Randall 1940, 20), is a very pessimistic reading of the possible solution to this problem. Instead, I propose a reconciliation between the city of God and the earthly city. In our age, it now becomes both possible and imperative for men to dwell simultaneously in their power and their love.

The roots of this reconciliation come from the era of the Fall, just as the roots of the hero-warrior and the hero-transcendent come from that era. The hero-creative manifests in the call of Yahweh to Abraham to be creative and bless the earth, in the call of Jacob to find the love of woman and blessing in fullness of earth's bounty, in the call of Moses to create a free people from a slave people. We find the struggle of the hero-creative in the development of the sciences and the arts, in bursts of creative outpouring such as the Renaissance. And we will find the beginning of his full manifestation in the stories of the quest for the Holy Grail. The remnants of dualistic patterns of thought continue to constrain us, however. We have not yet, fully as a culture, as a world, embraced the potential of becoming true cocreators with God of earthly life. The time is upon us when we must turn toward the hero-creative. We cannot live longer in the conflicts between the hero-warrior and the hero-transcendent.

The following dream reveals the possibility of the reconciliation for which we are seeking. It came to me the night of 4 October 1982. As I interpreted it, I saw the philanthropist/environmentalist representing a contemporary extension of the hero-transcendent in his efforts to preserve life and the business tycoon as a contemporary extension of the hero-warrior in his role of manipulation of earthly forms.

> There are two old men, both wise and spiritually mature. One is a philanthropist and environmentalist. The other is a business tycoon. They both live very high up in tall apartment buildings of the same height in a city. They are very good friends. It is clear that each has attained the height of spiritual wisdom. But the views they look upon from their apartments are very different. The philanthropist looks out over a park full of trees and greenery—the world of nature he has helped to preserve. The business tycoon looks out over the concrete of the city—the world he has helped to build.

The time has come for the two men in each of us to come to fullness, maturity, and friendship, lest we perish. Through their embrace and creative cooperation, not only will we not perish, but we will truly flourish and unleash a creative power for the renewal of the earth, as yet unknown.

Experiential Questions

1. Explore your relationship with nature. Do you think of yourself as a creature, related to all other creatures of earth? Do you think of yourself as separate from nature? Do you find yourself relating to both positions? How well do you relate to your body? Are you in touch with the stress signals your body gives out?

2. Matthew Fox (1983) speaks of the necessity of beginning our spiritual life in a positive relationship to the earth. How do you find sustenance in nature? What activities within nature and through your body do you find pleasurable and sources of energy?

3. How related are you to the destructive elements of natural life? Are you able to relate to the suffering that is inherent in earthly, human existence? Fox also speaks of the necessity for relating to the suffering that is a part of human life. How do you connect with earthly suffering?

4. The psychological theme of this chapter is that manhood requires us to separate from our mothers and from our family in a way analogous to the separation of human consciousness from nature that happened two to four thousand years ago. As you reflect on your answers to questions one through three above, how are your answers similar and different from your understanding of how your parents might answers those questions? In what ways, as you explore your relationship to nature, have you left your original home base and in what ways are your values similar to that home base?

5. Now turn to your relationship with your mother. How do you relate to her as source of your arrival and early sustenance in physical life? What qualities do you bring forward into your life from your relationship with your mother? What spiritual or creative tasks have you brought forward from your relationship with her? In what ways did your relationship with your mother lay the foundation for your current values? In what ways have you fought against your mother's values to establish your own?

6. In what ways do your relationships past and present with nature and with your mother influence your relationship with other women in your life?

7. What are the sources of deep nurturance for you at the present?

3

◆ ◆ ◆

THE HERO-WARRIOR

> The Lord is a warrior: the Lord is his name.
> The chariots of Pharaoh and his army
> he has cast into the sea:
> the flower of his officers
> are engulfed in the Red Sea.
> The watery abyss has covered them,
> they sank into the depths like a stone.
> Thy right hand, O Lord, is majestic in strength:
> thy right hand, O Lord, shattered the enemy.
> (Exod. 15: 3–6, NEB)

The deliverance of the slave people of Israel from Egypt was through the conflict of battle. The people celebrated that victory in song. God was a warrior to them. Furthermore, during the conquest of Canaan by the Hebrew people, their God was a god of war, inspiring the slaughter of thousands of people.

> After the death of Joshua the Israelites inquired of the Lord which tribe should attack the Canaanites first. The Lord answered, "Judah shall attack. I hereby deliver the country into his power." . . . The Lord delivered the Canaanites and Perizzites into their hands. They slaughtered ten thousand of them at Bezek. (Judg. 1:1–4, NEB)

In a similar vein, Scipio Africanus delivered a prayer of supplication to the gods of Rome as he was leading the Roman expedition to Carthage in 204 B.C.E. The following prayer is recorded in Livy's history of Rome:

> Ye gods and goddesses, who inhabit the seas and the lands, I supplicate and beseech you that whatever has been done under my command, or is being done, or will later be done, may turn out to my

advantage and to the advantage of the people and the commons of Rome . . . that you will grant that, preserved in safety and victorious over the enemy, arrayed in booty and laden with spoils, you will bring them back with me in triumph to our homes; that you will grant us the power to take revenge upon our enemies and foes; and that you will grant to me and the Roman people the power to enforce upon the Carthaginians what they have planned to do against our city, as an example of [divine] punishment. (Eliade 1967, 283)

The contents of this prayer have been offered countless times since, as one people set out on its "divinely" appointed quest for triumph over another people. The history of peoples since the times of these accounts is only too clear. The era of male ascendency has been filled with war and bloodshed. Whether we survey the history of Rome in its conquests, or its invasions by so-called barbarians, or the subsequent history of Europe, the history of Islam, or the battles for supremacy in the Americas or in Asia, the justifications for war include invocation of divine authority in causes of justice and in causes of expansion. The era of male ascendency has brought the harshest conflicts of humanity with itself, harsher conflicts than those evidenced in the animal kingdom. Humankind has evidenced the capacity for destruction side by side with its development of knowledge, art, and all forms of culture. Are there clues for us to understand this phenomenon and to address the capacity for aggressive destructiveness within ourselves? If so, what are the implications of these patterns of violence for men in our time?

Such questions pose issues far beyond the scope of any one discipline or one work. The questions have puzzled philosophers, theologians, and dramatists for centuries. We will not conclusively answer them in this chapter. What we will do, however, is explore themes from mythology that aid us in better understanding ourselves. We will look for clues to the development of the warrior mentality, and we will explore some of the implications of that mentality.

Although the hero-warrior is very powerfully manifest in the Hebrew scripture, we will turn to Greek mythology for our primary model to illumine the warrior aspect of the male soul. The male warrior that we encounter in mythology is well described in the story of Hercules. Hercules became the "champion of all Greece." His story is full of anecdotes that lend insight into the personality of the warrior and his legacy for our time. In that story we find a man with great capacity for service undertaken in noble causes. We also find Hercules learning new technological skills, so that he is able to address the beasts of nature and the tasks of war with increasingly sophisticated weapons. Unfortunately, we also find that, as a foreshadowing of our own time, these weapons take on a destructive power of their own. Even as early as the tale of Hercules, we find that humanity has fallen victim to its own technological power. The most destructive power, however, lies in Hercules' unbridled violence. In his story we encounter numerous circumstances in which a blind rage overtakes Hercules, and he destroys those whom he loves. These blind rages are tied to the revenge Hera is taking upon him. Thus, we find that the spurned feminine is taking revenge against the youthful male hero figure, as he seeks hegemony over the earth and over nature. We find him not yet fully liberated from the feminine and from nature. We find the hero-warrior still struggling to assert his independence.

We find a similar problem of blind rage in Achilles, who, in his final victory over Hector, falls victim to a rage that devours his own code of honor. So caught is he in violent energy of the battlefield that he cannot disengage himself from it. After the battle, his rage continues and he drags Hector's naked body around the walls of Troy. The warrior's code of honor would insist, instead, that he give respect to his foe in death. Only when Hector's father, Priam, begs for his son's body to be honored does Achilles come out of his rage. Then his anger becomes sorrow, and he returns to his senses and his code of honor, releasing Hector's body to Priam (Fields 1991, 73–74).

Thus there are many themes of the hero-warrior reflected in these mythic images, among them the commands of warrior gods, the parallel development of technological skill and weapons of destruction, and the nature of the warrior's violence, its training and its taming. The legacy of the hero-warrior for contemporary men is a tendency toward aggression that still calls for training and balance, and a technology that similarly calls for balance. Concurrent with these problems, however, is the warrior's capacity for self-sacrifice for noble causes, his capacity for dispensing justice, his willingness to serve his state and his god in the dissemination of his culture across new lands, and the capacity for abiding friendship with his comrades. There are warrior virtues. "If we are accessing the Warrior appropriately we will be energetic, decisive, courageous, enduring, persevering, and loyal to some greater good beyond our own personal gain" (Moore and Gillette 1990, 95).

We begin the exploration of the hero-warrior through the discovery that the warrior arises in human history concurrent with the ability to forge metals and develop technological skills.

Of Metals and Murder

The man lay with his wife Eve, and she conceived and gave birth to Cain. She said, "With the help of the Lord I have brought a man into being." Afterwards she had another child, his brother Abel. Abel was a shepherd and Cain a tiller of the soil. The day came when Cain brought some of the produce of the soil as a gift to the Lord; and Abel brought some of the first-born of his flock, the fat portions of them. The Lord received Abel and his gift with favour; but Cain and his gift he did not receive. Cain was very angry and his face fell. Then the Lord said to Cain, "Why are you so angry and cast down?

> If you do well, you are accepted;
> if not, sin is a demon crouching at the door.
> It shall be eager for you, and you will be mastered by it."

Cain said to his brother Abel, "Let us go into the open country." While they were there, Cain attacked his brother Abel and murdered him. Then the Lord said to Cain, "Where is your brother Abel?" Cain answered, "I do not know. Am I my brother's keeper?" The Lord said, "What have you done? Hark! Your brother's blood that has been shed is crying out to me from the ground. Now you are accursed, and banished from the ground which has opened its mouth wide to receive your brother's blood, which you have shed. When you till the ground, it will no longer yield you its wealth. You shall be a vagrant and a wanderer on the earth." (Gen. 4:1–12, NEB)

The tragic story of Cain and Abel is one that we have already heard in another form in the story of Romulus and Remus. The conflict for the two brothers begins in religious ritual. Romulus sees twelve vultures and Remus sees six vultures while they are making sacrifice to determine the location of Rome. Cain brings offerings from the land and is rebuked by God, while Abel's sacrifice of sheep is accepted. In the story of Cain and Abel the shepherding life of the Israelite people is given preference over the agrarian life of the

Canaanites, whose land they are to seize. The Hebrew God shows preference for the nomadic shepherds, just as he will scorn the mother goddess worship of the Canaanites. But there is also another clue to the arising of violence of brother upon brother in this story. Abel means "shepherd" and Cain means "smith" (Eliade 1978, 167). Cain is a blacksmith. He has learned to forge metal, to make tools for cultivating the land, and to make weapons of iron. Furthermore, in his exile, he becomes the builder of a city (Gen. 4:17). "So the first murder is performed by him who in some sort incarnates the symbol of technology and urban civilization" (Eliade 1978, 168). In both the story of Cain and Abel and the story of Romulus and Remus, violence goes hand in hand with the founding of cities and is an offspring of technology.

The precipitating factor in Cain's actions is the seeming rejection of his sacrifice by God, which creates anger in him. God answers his outburst of anger in a way that shows Cain, and his youthful male spirit, that he must become responsible for himself and learn to deal with his anger. Unfortunately, just as this anger poses a problem for Hercules and Achilles, Cain falls prey to its power. He is mastered by his unbridled anger and sets out to murder his brother. How will the aggressive power that seems to be brought forth in the hero-warrior be tamed? This issue, I suggest, is still very much with us as contemporary men. Will we draw back from our aggression and fail in the tasks of new creation or will we be so ruled by our aggression that we wreak havoc on those around us? How will the violence that erupts in thousands of households each day be tamed? Does the training and history of the hero-warrior give us any clues to our dilemmas?

The theme is so prevalent in the mythic record that I believe there are some clues for our contemporary problems. A story very similar to Cain's anger occurs in the tales of Hercules. In that story, Hera sends a madness upon Hercules during which he kills his children. Hera is the wife of Zeus, a prototype of the vengeful woman. Perhaps she represents the antagonism of the old feminine order which has been lorded over by the masculine. She envies Zeus's affairs with earthly women, and since Hercules is the son of one of these liaisons, she is vengeful toward him.

Hera . . . took advantage of this moment and changed his sullenness to savage frenzy. He became so utterly mad that he tried to murder his cherished nephew Iolaus, and when the boy managed to escape, shot the children Megara had borne him, imagining that he was aiming his arrows at the giants. It was a long time before his madness left him. But when he realized his terrible mistake, he was bowed down with grief, locked himself into his house, and refused to have anything to do with his fellow men. When time at last lessened his sorrow, he resolved to accept the labors of Eurystheus, and went to him at Tiryns, which was part of his kingdom. (Schwab 1946, 166)

Thus Hercules' famed Twelve Labors are undertaken to release him from the guilt of his destruction of his children. We see that these labors represent the effort of a struggling masculine consciousness and conscience to come to terms with violence and with unconscious forces. Cain premeditates the murder of his brother. Hercules performs murder in a blind rage, a fit of insanity. Yet who is more insane: Cain who is gripped by anger and wills his brother's death, or Hercules who loses all sense of self in his blind rage? The courts of our time find a difference. Yet from the standpoint of moral responsibility, is there a difference? Hercules repents of his crime and willingly enters into Zeus's will. Cain repents as well. In their repentence moral responsibility is born. Both Hercules and Cain become wanderers of the earth, entering into individual life apart from tribe or clan. They are forerunners of modern man in his isolation before God and his own moral responsibility. In the dawning awareness of self-consciousness, which is the Fall, humanity becomes aware that it possesses personal power and autonomy. However, we become aware also that our power is limited. Our power is less than the powers of the divine. In the cosmos, we are limited. What will we do with our limited power?

The extent of humankind's newly found power lies with the ability to shape the environment. The power of the smith, of Cain, is the newly found power of male consciousness. The potentiality and difficulty of this power is shown in the Greek version of the smith, Hephaestus. Hephaestus is the fallen god of Greek mythology. He was born of Hera to spite Zeus. When he was born he was deformed, lame in both feet. According to different legends, he was thrown out of Olympus by Zeus in anger, or he was thrown out by Hera because of his infirmity. In either case, he is the cast-off child. He is taken into a deep cave in the ocean and there becomes apprentice for nine years as a smith and artisan (Eliade 1978, 265). In Hephaestus, with his lame legs, we find humanity cast out of its alliance with nature and aware of its frailty. Humanity must depend on its own ingenuity. And in that ingenuity humanity begins to claim equality with the gods. Hephaestus becomes the master trickster of the Olympians. Through his skills in metallurgy, he is much in demand in Olympus. But he also does not hesitate to avenge himself and the indignities he has suffered. He is master artist and master "binder." "With his works—thrones, chains, nets—he binds gods and goddesses, as well as the Titan Prometheus" (ibid., 266). Hephaestus shows us humanity now with our newly found powers challenging the gods. In one episode, Hephaestus sends his mother, Hera, a golden throne. However, when she sits in it, it holds her captive. No god can free her. Dionysus is sent for and only through the power of wine is Hephaestus persuaded to free his mother.

In this anecdote, we see clearly many of the issues that face emerging male consciousness. With his power of artificial creation, Hephaestus revenges himself by binding up his mother, Hera. The image of the mother bound by the abused child is a powerful statement of the male in infancy in his newly found power, exercising that power against the feminine, whether that feminine be the earth or women or the often unspoken but deep chasm of anger that separates sons from mothers. He will not free her, and it is only through ecstatic intoxication, through contact with the transcendent aspect of his own masculine nature, that he is able to go beyond his revenge and release her. Here we find an issue that lurks behind the era of masculine ascendency, the theme of attaining power over nature. And it raises once again the question of what we will do with our anger over the abuses that nature and supernature heap upon us.

Most significant, however, is the ability of Hephaestus to intimidate the gods. Because of his powers of creation, he has assumed a dominion over both the earthly forms of matter and over the gods. We recall the powers given to St. Peter, the "keys" of heaven, the power to loose and to bind both on earth and in heaven. The power to work metal brings with it the responsibilities of binding and loosing. Technology evokes fear in the gods and power over other people. The ability to master fire and metals has given humankind the ability to wage war on an ever more massive scale.

Mastery over the Beasts

One of the major themes in mythology, in which we see male consciousness differentiating itself from nature, is the mastery over the beasts of the earth. This developing power in the hero of prehistory involves the cultivation of aggression and of warrior skills. Zeus, in his defeat of the Typhon, is the prototype of this struggle. The emerging masculine consciousness manifests as authority over nature. This theme, as manifest in Greek mythology, is very similar to the "dominion" over the earth given by the Hebrew God to Adam.

Fig. 8. Herakles Strangling the Nemean Lion, Psiax, height 19½", c. 525 B.C.E. (detail of attic black-figured amphora from Vulci). Museo Civico, Brescia.

The theme of mastery over the beasts is very strongly present in the early labors of Hercules. In these labors, he meets and overpowers threatening beasts, and he begins to develop technological power. These labors show a growing authority of humankind over nature. In the first labor he is sent to confront the Nemean lion (Figure 8). When Hercules enters the woods of Nemea, he can find no one in the countryside. All have fled from the lion or locked themselves inside their houses (Schwab 1946, 166). A beast has suddenly appeared in a region that was otherwise pastoral. Hercules' task is to clear the land of this menace of nature.

Buckminster Fuller offers a fascinating viewpoint on this particular problem. He suggests that in prehistory the ice ages created great upheavels in the natural order of pastoral life. Suddenly wild animals approached lands previously domesticated. The waterfront was lowered in the ice ages, creating landbridges where none existed before. Furthermore, many of the animals of more remote regions were pushed southward by the ice. He states that this is how animals like tigers got into island regions like Bali. Faced with this onslaught of animals, people who were previously pastoral farmers had to become aggressive to defend themselves. This phenomenon accounts in large measure for the development of aggressive social behavior in humankind. Aggression, according to Fuller, is a secondary characteristic of human behavior, only enlisted when humanity becomes desperate to achieve its basic needs. Fuller speaks of two basic kinds of human social behavior, benign and aggressive. He offers the speculation that the roots of these types can be found in the relationship of human societies to animals. Where humanity was not overwhelmed by animals, it learned to domesticate animals. Where the animals tended to overwhelm humanity, it developed aggressive tendencies, and the most aggressive learned to mount horses and pursue the animals (Fuller 1981, 66–67). These aggressive horsemen became one of the great warrior forces in human history.

Hercules' second labor continues to fit this schema. The hydra, a water beast, comes forth onto domesticated land. "It was her custom to crawl ashore to tear the cattle limb from limb and lay waste the fields" (Schwab 1946, 168). Here we may have a metaphor for tidal waves or other natural sea disasters. In any case, the disaster is a disruption of established domestic life. The hero-warrior is called upon to help restore order by his prowess as a predator. In the encounter with the hydra, Hercules becomes master of nature at a more advanced level than in his encounter with the Nemean lion. The skin of the Nemean lion was so tough that he had to use the claws of the lion to skin it. He has mastered the beast on its own terms, with its own weapons. However, after killing the hydra, Hercules dips his arrows into the venom of the beast. Furthermore, the beast is overcome by fire. And Hercules asks for help from his companion Iolaus. Iolaus has tended the fire and gives Hercules a torch at just the right moment to singe the many heads of the hydra. In the legend of the hydra, the hunter joins his aggressive skills with the technologies created by fire: the metal arrow. When Hercules further empowers his arrows by dipping them in the hydra's venom, the arrows become so lethal that they often inflict torment on innocents. And indeed, it is through this venom that Hercules is finally tormented into his suicide-sacrifice. That story jumps far ahead of our theme, however, so we will save it. The point I wish to make here is that legend blends with scholars of prehistory to paint a picture for the emerging aggressive nature of mankind and the additional responsibilities, possibilities, and grave dangers that technological skills provide.

The third labor of Hercules demonstrates humanity reaching for parity with nature. The task is to bring back the deer of Mount Cerynea. For a year she eluded Hercules. Finally, he wearied of the chase and wounded her in the leg, so that he might catch her to carry her back alive. While he has her on his shoulders, Hercules is met by Artemis and upbraided for planning to kill the creature. "'Great goddess,' said Hercules to justify himself to her, 'it was not idle sport which prompted me to do this, but sheer necessity. For how else could I fulfill the wish of Eurystheus?' These words calmed her anger, and he brought the hind alive to Mycenae" (Schwab 1946, 169).

Hercules seems exonerated here, but we may well wonder about Eurystheus's motivations. It was sheer necessity for Hercules, but was it sheer necessity for Eurystheus? Is it possible that, now that the hero-warrior has gained parity with nature, the earthly ruler has begun to evidence his greed? Has the abuse of nature by an empowered humanity begun?

In Hercules' next adventure, it becomes clear humanity has won its contest with nature. The old forms of worship of the Great Mother are at an end. Hercules is sent to retrieve another animal sacred to Artemis, the Erymanthian boar. The boar was sacred to Demeter, representing the old goddess worship and the worship of nature. When Hercules finds the boar, he merely chases it out of the bush and catches the "weary beast" (ibid., 170). In this encounter, the old feminine forms of worship, together with a full union with nature, are portrayed as weary. They have served their time and are now at an end.

The story of capturing the boar is secondary to an encounter that happens along the way. In quest of the boar, Hercules stops to visit his centaur friend, Pholus. The centaurs are legendary half-horse, half-human creatures. They demonstrate humanity's full equality with nature. The centaur is a creature who is at home in both the animal kingdom and in human society. While dining, Hercules asks for wine. Pholus opens wine that Dionysus has stored in his cellar. However, when the aroma of the wine wafts out of Pholus's cave, other centaurs enter to attack Hercules and Pholus to get at the wine. In this encounter we see an emerging split between a higher and lower nature. Some of the man-beasts choose the path of social discourse, hospitality, and culture. Some of the man-beasts choose aggression to serve their personal whims. In the ensuing battle, the tragedy of Hercules' weapons is manifest. In pursuit of the centaurs he inadvertently wounds another old friend, Chiron. And Pholus, in examining one of the arrows, drops it on his foot and is killed by its venom. Pholus dies. Chiron seeks to die, but because he is immortal, is left in eternal torment. Hercules buries Pholus and vows to send death to Chiron.

In Hercules' story we have arrived at the dilemmas of modern humanity. Hercules' and humanity's technology has given us authority over nature and has taken on a power of its own. Now that technology has its own power, adding any increased knowledge brings more danger and more life to the technology. The warrior is called upon to defend his friends. But even in that noble defense, he loses his friends due to the "overkill" of his technology. Accidents can be quite as detrimental as intentional warfare. And in certain circumstances, death becomes the liberator rather than the enemy.

The history of war ever since the era of prehistory recorded in Hercules' tales could be told as a process of increasingly sophisticated weaponry. This process has continued unabated until the present era. Only with the dawn of the nuclear age has the warrior seen the possibility that the increasing sophistication of weaponry might itself become a defense against war. When confronted by the impact of the nuclear bomb in Japan, General Douglas MacArthur predicted that technology would put an end to war (Ward 1992, 72). However, in the limited wars since that event, the combat soldier has continued to be aided and victimized by technological developments. In commenting on the increasing toll that advancing weaponry has taken on the contemporary combat soldier, a Vietnam veteran speaks of the trauma of the Vietnam War:

> The weaponry was more lethal than previous wars. The Russian-made AK-47 assault rifle was considered by the troops to be a better weapon than their own M-14 or M-16. Advanced weaponry coupled with the guerilla warfare tactics resulted in sudden and intense combat. The outcome of an ambush, one's survival, was often determined by fire superiority in the first few seconds of contact. A conversation with a friend could be reduced to morsels of flesh to be picked off one's face.

In order to survive, men had to be hyperalert, resulting in even more anticipatory anxiety than in previous wars. The increasing trauma of war from ever more sophisticated and deadly assault weaponry is hard to realize. (Scull 1989, 32)

The tale of Hercules provides an amazingly graphic moment in our human history, when the technology of human weapons begins itself to fill humanity with dread.

The centaur's being as half-beast, half-man vividly portrays humanity's problem and hope. Will we learn to love our animal nature and make peace with nature even while we learn to love those parts of our human consciousness that separate us from nature and give us dominion over nature? Dare we hope for such a benign existence, now that the forces of technological destruction have been unleashed?

Of Necessity and Aggression

We will leave Hercules aside for the moment, at the point at which his hero-warrior skills have turned against him, to explore some of the themes that have emerged regarding the hero-warrior training and mentality. Two themes have emerged, two distinct yet contributory characteristics of the hero-warrior. His roots can be traced to the hunter in prehistory, and his modern form can be traced to mastery over fire and metals, and the creation of weapons. In the case of the hunter, the aim of all aggressive training is not to master nature in the sense of subduing her, but instead to become a successful son of her, coequal with the beasts. With the invention of technology as an emergent capability of the rational mind, however, humanity enters into the potential of mastering nature, becoming king of the beasts. Hubris is born in the defeat of the hydra and displays itself in the accidental deaths of Pholus and Chiron.

Fuller states that "aggression is a secondary behavior of humans." There is a major discussion among ethnologists, biologists, and anthropologists regarding the nature of human aggression, whether it is learned or innate. An interesting discussion is given in a series of essays edited by Ashley Montagu entitled *Man and Aggression* (1973). Many of the essays offer views opposing Konrad Lorenz's widely read book *On Aggression* (1966). Lorenz's work and its companion works, such as Desmond Morris's *The Naked Ape* (1968), point toward innate characteristics of aggression within the human species, which mirror and build upon aggressive characteristics within the primates and other species. In contrast to this view of "innate depravity," Ashley Montagu states, "the fact is, that with the exception of the instinctoid reactions in infants to sudden withdrawals of support and to sudden loud noises, the human being is entirely instinctless" (1973, 11). Montagu and his colleagues are concerned that the popular view of humanity as full of aggressive tendencies becomes an excuse to be aggressive. We become murderers like Cain or Hercules, but without their remorse, because after all, all the evidence points toward the inevitability of such aggressive behavior. To that postulation, Montagu offers the following rebuttal:

> Everything points to the non-violence of the greater part of early man's life, to the contribution made by the increasing development of cooperative activities, the very social process of hunting itself, the invention of speech, the development of food-getting and food-preparing tools, and the like. . . . When man hunts he is the predator and the hunted animal is prey. But prehistoric man did not hunt for pleasure, in order to satisfy his "predatory instincts." He hunted for food, to satisfy his hunger, and the hunger of those who were dependent upon him. (ibid., 6–7)

Montagu joins many anthropologists in asserting a long period of prehistory, in which tribes lived essentially a life in cooperation with nature and with one another in cohesive social units. Nevertheless, we know that whether aggression is instinctual or learned, it certainly does exist and has dominated Western culture, including the present century.

Lorenz offers a very useful position on the problem of aggression, regardless of our position on the innate or learned issue. Lorenz's position is based upon the observations that, within animal species apart from humanity, there are intraspecies safeguards against aggression. Aggression serves to produce the strongest male leader or to protect territorial feeding grounds within the species. However, each species has also evolved a retreat and submission signal, so that the one submitting to the strength of the other can retreat before being killed. If such killing accidentally takes place, the one who has killed the other will often show remorse, much as Hercules did after his blind killing of his children. According to Lorenz, weapons have allowed man to put distance between himself and the other person to the extent that the biological inhibitors cannot operate. The person using the modern weapon can press a button without realizing the emotional consequence to persons. "The deep, emotional layers of our personality simply do not register the fact that the crooking of the forefinger to release a shot tears the entrails of another man" (1966, 234). The same technological skills that freed humanity from dependency upon nature have also freed us from the natural inhibitors to aggression. Weapons put distance between man and man on the battlefield, enough distance that he could call one of his own species "enemy."

And what is it that this technician-warrior serves? It is an ever more complex civic structure. His society, his tribe, his family become his nation, gathered around certain principles, certain rules of life. God the Father was also the lawgiver and judge. If weapons increased the warrior's capability for extension of his personal power, then he has seemingly thought that he should increase his hegemony as far as his weapons and technology would take him. Empires are built on the premise that a people has a right, a "divinely" ordained obligation, to extend its beliefs and practices as far as its technology will allow it to extend. So, Scipio Africanus prays to the Roman gods for safe passage to extend *their* hegemony into Carthage. The Israelites hear God calling them to extend their authority into Canaan. We must recognize that at the roots of the masculine era of ascendency are male gods of war: Zeus, Yahweh, Odin. Is it possible that the power of a rising rational mind mistook the necessity to come to parity with nature for an aggressive right to subdue nature, and mistook the laws of its own culture for universal laws to be enforced upon every culture, and mistook the ability to create weapons for the license to use them?

. Beyond those deep questions is the historical evidence that aggression continues, whether or not it continues to serve humanity's survival as a species. The roots of the aggression that we men, particularly in American culture, feel or do not feel within ourselves is an issue of concern. Our prisons are filled with men who have acted in violence, and our middle-class homes are filled with those who have not been found out. Our culture asks us to go to war on demand and to be compliant citizens upon return home. And by and large, we have failed in the task in recent years. How can the historic and mythic evidence of the life of the hero-warrior assist us to make peace with ourselves?

The Hunter-Warrior

In the prehistory of humankind, men were hunter-gatherers for more than a million years. Anthropologists theorize that one of the primary reasons that the evolving humanoid species became so successful involved a division of labors between males and females. Our closest relatives in the animal kingdom, the chimpanzees, do not evidence such a division of responsibility. Among the chimps, a mother cares for one infant at a time because she is responsible for feeding both herself and her offspring. According to this theory, humanoid species began to divide the labors more efficiently. Men became food-gatherers; women were therefore able to care for more than one child at a time. The time a child was dependent on parents could be lengthened. Such increased period of childhood dependency also allowed the brain to evolve into greater complexity. A further factor was the change of our humanoid ancestors' sexual practices. Humankind is the only mammal to allow for constant sexual expression. In all other species, the female initiates sexual activity and it occurs only when the female is estrous. Human sexual activity is potentially available at any time. According to the theory we are suggesting, the reward for the males to be constantly engaged in hunting-foraging activities was the availability of sexual release at any time, which also began to create the specific bonding leading eventually to lifelong marriage patterns (Leakey and Lewin, 1977).

The Cultivation of Aggression

According to such a theory of human development, it was absolutely essential for man to become a proficient food-gatherer. His weapons enabled him to become a more effective hunter. It does not really matter in such a schema whether humanity inherited more aggressive or benign tendencies from the animal kingdom. Men found themselves needing to develop aggressive tendencies in order to survive. Just as the aggressive tendencies of Hercules served to clear the countryside of the terrors of the Nemean lion, so man's aggressive tendencies were useful in providing a safe territory and ample food for his growing family.

A survey of initiation rituals from tribal communities indicates that becoming a man often involved training of aggressive powers.

The "berserkers" evidenced such an initiation. They were the ancestor warriors of the European peoples. It is from these men, whose name meant "warriors in the shirts (serkr) of bear," from which our word *berserk* has derived. There is a famous passage from the *Ynglingasaga* that describes these men: "They went without shields, and were mad as gods or wolves, and bit on their shields, and were as strong as bears or bulls; men they slew, and neither fire nor steel would deal with them; and this is what is called the fury of the berserker" (Eliade 1967, 294).

There is ample evidence in many cultures of such training in aggression and identification with the animal to be hunted. Such initiation rituals were described as long ago as in the writings of Tacitus, who describes a people called the Chatti. Each youth to be initiated into manhood among the Chatti left his hair and beard uncut until he had killed an enemy. In many early European groups, the initiation into manhood came about through identification with the wolf and the initiation into secret men's societies. "By putting on the skin, the initiand assimilated the behaviour of a wolf; in other words, he became a wild-beast warrior, irresistible and invulnerable; 'Wolf' was the appellation of the members of the Indo-European military societies" (ibid., 294-96).

Such rituals have been documented among contemporary tribal peoples. A remarkable account of the customs of a tribe in the Amazon is reported by Manuel Córdova-Rios in experiences during the early part of the twentieth century. Although the precise authenticity of his account has been questioned (Carniero 1980), it nevertheless reveals practices typical of Amazon tribes. The tribe prepares for battle:

> Our preparations ended with a ceremony that put us all in a fight frenzy. We sat around a large circle, and as a small clay pot was passed around each dipped his forefinger into the mixture in the pot and then licked his finger. From the taste, the basic ingredient of this liquid preparation was tobacco, but there were other ingredients I did not know.
>
> The effect, after a few rounds, was heightened nervous agitation and tension. Talk of battle and of what would be done to our present annoyers prevailed. And when an individual could stand the tension no longer he would jump to the middle of the circle to give a loud wild demonstration of what he would do to any enemy that came within his reach. The fervor and frenzy were contagious—working

back and forth around the circle. And the displays of individual violent aggressiveness were awesome.

Late in the afternoon when the chief could hold them no longer, we prepared to depart. (Lamb 1974, 82)

Here, preparations for a specific battle resemble the general training of the berserker. Another account demonstrating the arousing of tremendous aggressive behavior is reported by Livy in his history of Rome. In this account, the Romans were battling the Latins around 340 B.C.E. The Romans began to lose ground. Decius decided to make an offering of himself in order to turn the tide of battle.

Then, girding himself with the Gabinian cincture and leaping, armed, upon his horse, he plunged into the thick of the enemy, a conspicuous sight to both armies and with something about him more august than human, as though he had been sent from heaven to expiate all the anger of the gods, and to avert destruction from his people and turn it upon their enemies. Thus the greatest terror and dread accompanied him, and, throwing the Latin front into disorder, it at once spread deeply into their whole army. This was most clearly evident from the fact that wherever he rode, men trembled as if struck by some baleful star; and when he fell beneath a hail of missiles, in that instant there could be no doubt of the consternation of the Latin cohorts, which everywhere deserted the field and took to flight. At the same time the Romans—their spirits now set free from religious fears—pressed on as if only then the signal had been given for the first time, and delivered a united blow. (Eliade 1967, 225)

The problem of such martial training that equips men to become equal to aggressive carnivores in order to go to battle is well illustrated by the old Irish story of Cuchulainn. In youthful fury he set off to conquer the three sons of Necht, the worst enemies of Ulster. He was successful, but his fury had been raised to such a pitch that a witch warned he would kill all the warriors of Ulster if he were not soothed. The king first sent naked young women to meet him. But he looked on his chariot instead of the women. Finally, he was lifted into three vats of water to cool him. "The first burst its staves and its hoops like the cracking of nuts around him. The next vat into which he went boiled with bubbles as big as fists therein. The third vat into which he went, some men might endure it and others might not" (ibid., 296). Only when his fury had thus been cooled was his accomplishment celebrated.

From the standpoint of current male issues, the evidence that aggression has been systematically drilled into us for the preservation of the species means that there resides within us the capacity for tremendous aggression. A forty-four-year-old construction worker and draftsman reported the eruption of such primitive power during an incident almost twenty years before. His daughter was an infant. He and his wife were at the limits of their endurance. The girl had been ill for several days. He had agreed to feed her in the night. At the 3:00 A.M. feeding time, she was crying. There was nothing that he seemed to be able to do to stop her crying. He suddenly felt his whole body trembling with rage. He knew in that moment that he could have destroyed his daughter. He resisted his rage. However, he has been fearful of this aggressive power within himself ever since.

A problem that men thus face is to contact this deep source of strength and power, and to learn how to control and channel it. In tribal cultures in which such aggressive powers were cultivated, there were also socially prescribed ways for discharging aggression. Córdova-Rios describes a festival after the return of the men from a successful trading excursion. A celebration began, with painting of their bodies in original designs. Then dancing began, which went on for several days. After drinking and dancing for more than a day, brawls and pushing contests began to happen among the men. However, the chief would always step in if a situation began to become dangerous. The chief was given full respect by every man, and thus none of these conflicts became harmful (Lamb 1974, 112–14). Here, mild displays of aggression are used in a controlled way to "let off steam." The warriors, who have been trained with fully awakened aggression when needed, also have a socially sanctioned way to deal with disputes among themselves. There is a pattern within the culture for aggression and its release.

The Cultivation of Perception and of Discipline

The hunter-warrior must have discipline as well as structured release of the aggressive powers his training has evoked. Such discipline allows the chief to have respect and authority to check intratribal aggressions. Such discipline allows for the self-sacrifice of Decius. One form of discipline for the hunter is the disciplining of body and senses in order to perceive the environment with great detail. The cultivation of perception is essential to the hunter, whether of animals or as the warrior in battle. Córdova-Rios describes extensive training in perception of the prey to be hunted by the Amazonian tribe. Minute details of each bird, including their nesting habits, mating dances, and all their songs and sounds are studied, so that the hunter can be successful in his observation and ultimate attack of the prey (Lamb 1974, 92–93). The cultivation of this observing capacity creates the climate for humanity's development of technology. The hunter-warrior has contributed enormously to the development of the discipline of sensory observation through the million years of his existence.

In the later labors of Hercules, we find him disciplining himself and cultivating the power of perception sufficiently to fashion sophisticated technology to deal with specific problems. We return to his story following the incident in which his weapons have assumed a lethal power of their own. The next labor is potentially one of great humiliation. He is to clear the stables of Augeas in a single day. Three thousand cattle had been kept there for a long time. "When the demigod stood in the presence of Augeas and offered to perform this service, without however mentioning that it was at the command of Eurystheus, the king measured this stalwart youth in his lion's skin and could hardly suppress laughter at the thought that so noble a warrior could wish to do the task of a common servant" (Schwab 1946, 171).

By blending his observation of nature with his technological skill, Hercules completes the task. He builds a canal and turns the waters of the rivers Alpheus and Peneus into the canal to clean out the stables. By submitting to this humiliating task, Hercules evidences a growing discipline to match his strength and his weapons. He uses his sense perception and engineering skills in this task rather than simply his aggressive power.

In the next labor, there is an awakening of even higher knowledge. He is asked to clear the region of the Stymphalian birds. As Hercules ponders this problem, the goddess Pallas Athene appears to him in a vision and gives him enormous bronze rattles fashioned by Hephaestus with which to scare away the birds. Here a new development evidences. A higher rationality, symbolized by the goddess, now equips Hercules to use weapons specifically fashioned for this task. He shows us humanity learning to use the metallurgic skill in addressing specific problems in nature. Hercules makes a tremendous sound with the rattles and scares the birds into flight. He kills them with his arrows while they are flying.

Several other labors share the common theme of taming the wild beast. In one case, he tames the Minoan bull who rages madly. In another, he must tame the mares of Diomedes of Thrace. These mares are so strong and savage that they prefer to feed on human flesh and must be subdued. In another labor, he must fight Geryon for his oxen. Geryon is a huge monster with three bodies, three heads, six arms, and six feet. In each of these quests there is the theme of mastering the beast. If we view the story now as descriptive of human evolution, we may be at the point where the tremendous energies of aggression, carefully trained in men for the protection of their clans, must now also be confronted and disciplined. In each case Hercules succeeds. His own disciplined strength, however, must continue to be present in the case of the Minoan bull and the mares of Diomedes. When he is not present, they revert to their destructive power. Humanity stands between the constructive and destructive uses of its aggressive powers. The warrior must be vigilant, lest he inadvertently unleash his trained aggression and kill the innocents.

The potential for evil, as a force that manifests seemingly of its own accord, has appeared in the increased technology of Hercules' weapons. Now evil manifests as willful deception in Hercules' encounter with the Amazons. Hercules' task is to bring back the girdle of Hippolyte, the queen of the Amazons. The girdle was a gift to her from Mars. Hercules discusses the matter with her, and she agrees to give it to him. Here we encounter the potential for negotiations to settle disputes. Reason is in place, discourse can happen, and all seems well. However, Hera intervenes, disguises herself as an Amazon, and spreads a false rumor that Hercules is about to abduct their queen. The Amazons attack Hercules and many people are killed. The picture of human life presented in this episode seems very familiar to us. Within this story lies the potential for rational solution to conflict and the quagmire of irrational forces leading us on to armed aggression. If we examine the themes that have thus far evidenced in Hercules' story, we discover modern consciousness.

Modern Consciousness and the Hero-Warrior

Hercules has demonstrated a growing capability throughout the labors. In the first labor he uses his brute strength, his hunter aggression, and his hunter skills to destroy the Nemean lion. In the second labor his own skills are aided by the mastery of fire, the creation of his weapons, and the increased lethalness of his weapons by his use of the hydra's venom. He begins soon to pay for this added skill. In the deaths of his centaur friends, by the careless use of his lethal weapons, Hercules discovers to his dismay that his weapons have taken on their own power to destroy. Subsequent labors illustrate the cultivation of discipline to match his formidable aggressive power. In addition, a higher rationality in the form of Pallas Athene has manifested. Through this intelligence, he is able to make great advances in technology and to destroy the parts of nature that pose a threat to his existence. He has learned engineering skills in diverting the rivers to his purposes. What he has not done, however, is learn to cope with Hera. The indomitable forces of the unconscious seem ever present, disrupting his control and discipline, and causing him to be victimized by his raw aggressive power. Suddenly, without warning, Hera can appear and undo his negotiated settlements. Reason has its limits. Male consciousness as it has developed has its tragic flaw. There is a part of the male soul that is lost, represented by these episodes of vengeance that Hera brings upon Hercules. Further stories of his adventures contribute to understanding of our contemporary dilemmas.

The hero-warrior has been concerned preeminently with the mastery over the world of sense. Through his sense perception, carefully honed during millennia of life as a hunter-gatherer, he has learned to see nature and to master it through more and more advanced technologies. The scientific revolution of the last two centuries is essentially a revolution based on increasing facility in sense perception, with ever more refined telescopes, microscopes, and other forms of observation. His goddess is Pallas Athene, preeminently the goddess of technology. We seem to have a man full of aggressive capabilities, checked by discipline, and equipped with the tools of rationality. His nemesis, however, is an unconscious propensity to sudden outbursts of uncontrolled violence.

A part of the resolution of the suffering that hangs so heavily over both Hercules and the modern hero-warrior in his love affair with weapons of ultimate destruction lies in an exploration of Hercules' relationship with the feminine. The similarity of the names *Hercules* and *Hera* gives us a clue. Hercules' life is dominated by his relationship with Hera, although Hera is not his natural mother. When he was an infant, he was abandoned, and Hera and her companion found him. For one brief moment, Hera nursed Hercules. Suddenly she sensed Hercules' strength and knew who he was. She pushed him away from her breast. However, in that moment of nursing, she had passed on immortality to him.

In the correlations we have been exploring between human development and mythic history, this story in mythology illustrates the period of late infancy for the male infant. There is a symbiotic relationship between mother and son, in which the child "tastes" unity with the mother during the course of nursing. That unitive bliss of infancy is a foretaste of transcendent radiance, which we may discover in maturity and in death. However, for the male child, it will mean that we are eternally bonded to our earthly mothers through a spiritual experience of unity. Hercules' adventures, while imposed by Hera, also keep him bound to her. As we will explore when we examine Hercules' death, there is an element there of his return to Hera through self-destruction. In some sense, Hercules presents to us a man full of strength who is still bound to his maternal figure. The problem for him, and perhaps for all of us men, is not that there is such an alliance for us with the one who has borne us and nursed us, but that we repress this bond and push it underground. The longing for such a nestling experience of softness haunts us. In Hercules' story that longing shows up as fits of rage that become fits of madness. He reminds us of one unable to move beyond temper tantrums. When he does not get what he wants, he lashes out in violence. Perhaps what he actually longs for is the discovery of a new form of relationship to the earthly, maternal matrix. He longs to discover a way in which earthly life may still be as nourishing as it was at the breast, a way which does not always require labors of him.

Hercules has bouts with madness brought on by Hera in stories other than those contained within the twelve labors. In one story, he at last seeks to be redeemed from this madness. The murder of Iphitus, in one of his fits, has weighed heavily upon him. He goes to the temple of Apollo at Delphi and seeks an oracle. But the priestess withholds healing from him. In response to this rebuke, Hercules steals her tripod and carries it out into a field to set up his own oracle. Apollo challenges Hercules to combat. Zeus intervenes, not wanting the brothers to fight, and Hercules is told that he must sell himself into slavery for a period of three years, sending the price of his service to the father of the slain Iphitus. Hercules sells himself into the service of Omphale in the Orient. Eurytus, the father, receives the money and distributes it to the children of Iphitus. Hercules is immediately cured for the rest of his life from his fits of violence. Direct compensation for the crime is made to Iphitus's family. Such increasing responsibility for his actions may contribute to Hercules' cure. But there is a very interesting twist to the story. In the service of Omphale, "in the sumptuous life of the Orient, [Hercules] forgot the teachings Virtue had once given him at the crossroads. He became voluptuous and effeminate" (Schwab 1946, 189). Hercules' cure involves becoming feminine! For three years, he dresses in women's clothes and lives softly!

In his encounter at the crossroads before beginning his heroic adventures, Hercules had met two women, Virtue and Idle Pleasure. He had chosen the path of Virtue. Now in his healing, he lives the life of Idle Pleasure. The path of Virtue which Hercules had chosen is given this description:

> "Know then that the immortals grant nothing to men without effort and toil. If you would have the gods look upon you kindly, you must honor them. If you would have your friends love you, you must aid them. If you would be held in esteem by a city, you must render it services. Would you have all Greece admire you for your virtue, you must become the benefactor of all Greece. If you would harvest, you must sow, if you would wage war and win, you must learn the art of warfare. If you would have control of your body, you must work and sweat to harden it." (ibid., 159)

In contrast, Idle Pleasure had offered a life of ease. "'My friends call me Happiness, but my foes, to humiliate me, have given me the name of Idle Pleasure'" (ibid.). She had offered an easy and sensuous path.

Now in an ironic and perhaps deeply wise twist in the story, Hercules is cured of the fits of madness by becoming idle and self-indulgent for a period of three years. Not only that, but he adopts the clothes of women and takes up spinning. In this healing may reside a very deep yearning within the soul of the hero-warrior. If we have painted an accurate picture of the prehistory of humanoid species, we have been sexually differentiated in regard to roles for well over a million years. Surely, deep within the soul of the hunter lies a longing to be more involved in the home, more concerned with child care, more involved in domestic chores. Just as surely in the female soul lies the hero-warrior yearning for self-expression in the contest with the world. Hera, after all, is preeminantly the goddess of home, hearth, and women.

In his warrior adventures, Hercules was prone simply to drag his family along. After his cure, he did successfully marry. He was no longer given to fits of madness, but he was still careless. In one of his journeys, he inadvertently killed a boy handing him a bowl of water to wash before dinner. He had to flee the region. So, his wanderings continued, now with his wife and his son, Hyllus, accompanying him. It is hard to see too much difference between Hercules' moving pattern and that of contemporary society in which male career considerations prevail in family decisions.

A predominant theme that emerges from our discussion is that the male has been trained to the life of adventurous conquest, whether of the civic sort or of warfare. He has not been well trained in domestic life. His task as provider is one with millennia of historic precedent. To complement that task with equal attention to home, hearth, and intimacy with spouse is a new role for men to undertake. We may find courage to explore our "softness" in Hercules' cure. For him, to be idle and indulgent for a period of time was a necessary part of his healing. It is not unreasonable to speculate that certain high-risk diseases for males, such as heart disease, hypertension, and strokes, may be related to this pattern of aggressive "virtue." Virtue's noble statement also has a dangerous quality about it: "The immortals grant nothing to men without effort and toil." Effort without rest, however, breeds Hercules' madness.

Another dominant theme in Hercules' story is his lack of companionship. His story is the hero in individual struggle. He rarely calls on companions for aid. When he does, as in the case of the hydra, the labor is not counted by Eurystheus, and he must perform another one alone. Hercules has no lifelong male companion. He has a series of companions, and in his fit of madness, he even kills one of these, Iphitus. In this respect, Hercules is very different from the tribal hunter-gatherers. Our prehistoric male ancestors, whose primary function would have been hunting or planting, would have done so in socially bonded groups. Hunter-gatherers would be bonded as the Amazon tribe cited by Córdova-Rios. While the individual hunted, he was also powerfully allied with his companions. In Hercules' model, the Western emphasis on individualism is powerfully exhibited. He is man, alone before his own psychic struggles, his awakened sense of justice, and his tasks of disciplined service. He is also alone in his madness with his blind aggression. He is a powerful mirror for contemporary Western men, who often do not develop strong bonds even with those with whom they work. Hercules' isolation points to a task that we must each recapture for ourselves, the possibility of brotherhood with other men.

Hope for a new form of companionship is exhibited in the story of Hercules and Admetus. In that story, Hercules has come into Admetus's home and gotten drunk. He knows that there has been a death, but because Admetus did not want to disturb Hercules' good spirits, he did not tell him that it is his wife, Alcestis, who has died. When Hercules discovers that it is his friend's wife who has died, he is filled with remorse. He wants to make amends for abusing his host's hospitality. He journeys into the underworld and retrieves Alcestis, motivated by friendship. Admetus blesses him for this feat. Themes of loyalty, of discipline, of justice predominate in Hercules' stories. To be sent on his way with love is not so frequent.

Spirituality by Theft

Hercules' final labors involve journeys into both the underworld and the upperworld. They are very instructive in regard to his spiritual capacity and the spiritual capacity of the egoic consciousness that he represents. We discover that both of these realms must be entered through deceit. They, so to speak, are not Hercules' by right.

Hercules is instructed to steal the guardian of the underworld, Cerberus. In this task Hercules successfully encounters the reality of death. He makes his way to Hades, the realm of the dead, and after great struggle succeeds in stealing Cerberus and bringing him out into the light of day. Cerberus "had three dog-heads with gaping jaws always slobbering venom, his body ended in a dragon's tail, and the hairs on his heads and his back were writhing snakes" (Schwab 1946, 180). Along the way, Hercules "fell upon Pluto's herds and slaughtered one of the oxen, in order to quench the thirst of the souls of the dead with blood" (ibid., 181). In this labor we can discern humanity's struggle with its dawning consciousness of death. Cerberus is another terrible aspect of earthly life, death itself. And the sacrificial offerings needed to quiet the souls of the dead are given by Hercules. Hercules' theft of Cerberus makes the separation between earthly life and the underworld less formidable. His ability to enter into the underworld demonstrates that humanity is shaping its identity by struggling with the fact of death and depth. Here Hercules brings us to the moment of existential dread. And he brings us to the question that has dominated Western spirituality: "Who shall deliver us from sin and death?"

It is interesting to note that Hercules does not enter into the upperworld until his death. He is sent on the labor to steal the golden apples of the Hesperides. These are the apples of the tree of life. These apples have been the gift of Gaia (the earth) to Zeus and Hera at the time of their marriage.

> On the western shore of the ocean she brought forth a tree with many boughs, all laden down with golden apples. Four virgins, the Hesperides, daughters of Night, were set to watch the sacred garden in which the tree grew, and they were aided in their task by Ladon, the hundred-headed dragon. (ibid., 177)

So, here in Greek legend is the same tree of life as grew in the Garden of Eden, the same serpent guardian, and the same promise of the eternal bounty of the earth. We shall find access to this tree in our chapter on the hero-creative. What is of interest in Hercules' story is that he does not himself enter the realm of this tree. Instead, he shoulders the world for Atlas, and sends Atlas to fetch the apples.

Along the way to Atlas, Hercules has also ended the use of human sacrifice as a form of worship to Zeus and freed Prometheus from his bondage. I find in these labors very powerful statements for the psychological work that we must each fulfill before the tree of life and its golden apples become available to us. The way of the Western hero will be to free the mind from its self-imposed shackles of guilt. It must awaken from any remaining dependence on sacrificial ritual. And it must release itself from the bondage of any guilt attached to the attainment of knowledge. Then, like Hercules, we must each learn to shoulder the world. And that is as far as the story of Hercules takes us. He himself does not venture into the garden of life. His story leaves that venture for later generations. However, he gives us the method of the West for attainment of the tree. Access to the golden reward is through the taking on of active responsibility in the world. It is by becoming coequal with nature and with all the powers and principalities that the more subtle spiritual realms will be opened. The hero of the West will learn to dwell in the material world as a means of unlocking the treasures of the spiritual world.

In Hercules' release of humanity from human sacrifice and of Prometheus from his eternal punishment, these Greek stories reveal a striking resemblance to the saga of Abraham in Hebrew tradition. Abraham is called upon to go forth to a new land and to become the progenitor of a new race. He is called upon to manifest the primary characteristic of God, the generative, creative aspect. In his saga, he finds himself at first hearing God ask for the sacrifice of his son Isaac. Only in the act of fulfilling this ancient form of human worship does he hear God calling for an end to human sacrifice. With both Hercules and Abraham, the ancient code of human subjugation to the divine through human sacrifice is ended. That Hercules frees Prometheus indicates a courage for human beings to begin to stand in personal moral responsibility with their newfound powers of fire and technological skill. In this task of personal moral responsibility, Hercules takes his place as a brother of Abraham and the other Hebrew Patriarchs.

Major themes for men that emerge from our discussion of the hero-warrior as seen through Hercules' labors are issues of intimacy with both men and women, the capacity to be in touch with one's aggressive capability—learning to use it and to discipline it—and the complementary capacity for softness and feminine receptivity. His story also shows us that his mentality cannot yet claim as his birthright the privilege of dwelling in the garden of the tree of life. Another theme is of a corporate nature. Where do we find the ceremonial opportunities to celebrate individual victories and to release the physiological stress of aggressive behavior?

The Death of Hercules and the Birth of Tragedy

Hercules' death epitomizes the tragic and yet transcendent possibilities of the warrior's life. Hercules does not die the victor's death on the battlefield. He dies as a victim of his own weapons. His death occurs as a tragic consequence of his wife's love for him, combined with the life force his weapons have taken on.

The story begins with Hercules' revenge. He has set out, after the completion of the twelve labors and the conclusion of his service to Eurystheus, to avenge himself against those who have wronged him. His final story turned toward "Eurytus, king of Oechalia, for whom he cherished an ancient grudge for having refused him his daughter Iole" (Schwab 1946, 196). The expedition is successful, and Hercules brings back Iole as a captive. When Deianira, Hercules' wife, discovers that Iole, his old flame, is under their roof, she worries about Hercules' faithfulness.

On another expedition, Hercules had shot a centaur with his poisoned arrow, because he seemed to be about to abduct Deianira. In revenge the centaur had told Deianira to take the liquid from his wound and keep it in a vial. At some point, in order to assure Hercules' undying love, she should wash his cloak in the liquid. The liquid was, of course, the poison from Hercules' arrow. Now in anxiousness, Deianira follows the centaur's advice. She sends a beautiful cloak to Hercules on the day of his offering of twelve bullocks to Zeus. The pyre is prepared. Hercules ascends wearing the new cloak, when its deadliness becomes apparent. The cloak sears itself into his back; he cannot remove it. He is locked in eternal torment. Hyllus, their son, rushes home enraged to berate his mother for sending the deadly cloak. When she hears the story, she withdraws and takes her own life, "a double-edged sword in her breast" (Schwab 1946, 200). Hyllus becomes the bearer of bad tidings yet a second time, telling Hercules the truth about Deianira's good intentions. When he heard that she had never intended for the cloak to wound him and had killed herself in remorse, Hercules' anger turned to sorrow. He betrothed Iole to Hyllus. He then set himself toward his death. An oracle from Delphi had once declared that he would die on Mount Oeta. He had himself carried there and placed upon a funeral pyre. His friend Philoctetes at last agreed to set the fire ablaze and in gratitute Hercules gave him his bow and poisoned arrows.

The tragedy manifests because, no one, not even Hercules, could withstand his weapons. Here in ancient myth is the dilemma facing contemporary humanity with the creation of the nuclear arsenal. Ultimate war, on behalf of well-intentioned values, will bring self-destruction. And at the day-to-day level of loves, jealousies, and quarrels between friends and lovers, we find the homicidal frenzy that often turns momentary anger into murder, because a weapon is handy. The question before humanity is whether, out of love and loyalty, we will unwittingly unleash our own weapons, which no one can withstand.

Hercules' death, however, is not without its transcendent aspect. When the pyre is lighted, lightning flashed from the sky and Hercules was borne away to Mount Olympus. From that time forward, he was worshiped in Greece as a deity. On Olympus, he was even reconciled to Hera. She gave Hercules her daughter Hebe as wife, and they bore children together and lived eternally. The honoring of the warrior's death is a very ancient tradition. Figure 9, a dying warrior, was created as part of a temple in Greece, erected around 500 B.C.E.

Hercules wins immortality, is reconciled to Hera, and becomes the champion of all Greece. There lies in this tragedy the seed of the hero-transcendent, whose path in life is a quest for the Eternal. We shall have much more to say about that in the following chapter. Here I would like to examine the story as the final outcome of the hero-warrior.

It is suggested in the story of Decius, who gave himself in sacrifice on behalf of the Romans, that there is honorable death and immortality accorded to the warrior. In Hercules' story, although the death comes through a series of miscalculations, the honorable death is nevertheless given. It is no secret that the Valkyrie of the Norsemen awaited the warriors to bring them into the realm of the dead. Man has not only deemed his warfare necessary, he has sanctified it. The battlefield has become a grandly numinous and holy place. In ancient cultures as diverse as the Celts mentioned by Julius Caesar, the Romans themselves, and ancient India, warriors were one of the most honored classes.

In order to free ourselves from the destructiveness of the warrior, we must also understand his historic function, which has been to provide peace *within* the borders of his sovereignty, for his clan, group, or nation. We must also understand the honor of dying on behalf of this sociopolitical unit, which has often meant dying for one's god as well. The dangers of not coming to terms with this historic warrior are immense.

An element of danger that emerges from both Hercules and from Decius is the suicidal element of the warrior. In the name of honor, Decius's suicide becomes a hero's death. To end eternal torment, Hercules' death seems both justified and most welcomed. In either case, there is an element of sacrifice. Furthermore, Deianira is praised by her son Hyllus for taking her life to "atone for her thoughtless act by inflicting death upon herself" (Schwab 1946, 200). Are we, in the warrior's honoring of death, in the realm of atonement to the gods? And if so, what is it for which humanity must continue to atone?

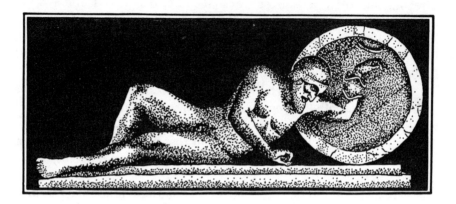

Fig. 9. Dying Warrior. Marble, length 72″, c. 490 B.C.E., from the east pediment of the temple at Aegina. Glyptothek, Munich.

In *Up From Eden* (1981b), Ken Wilber speaks of murder, suicide, and warfare as "substitute sacrifices." The real sacrifice that life wants of us is the dissolving of boundaries, the release from artificial disruptions of the unity that underlies all reality. The ultimate sacrifice is not surrender to the clan or nation, but surrender into the unity of all living creatures. In clinging to his loyalty to clan and nation, the warrior finds a form of transcendence via his own death. But Wilber suggests that the real death that life desires of us is not this sacrifice of our physical lives, but the surrender of the hero's boundaries, his effort to maintain individuality and clan loyalty at all costs.

> It hardly needs to be said, but it does follow that transcendence, true transcendence, is the only cure for the homicidal animal. If, in killing, all man wants is to kill, then we are all in deep trouble. The kill wish is ultimate and ineradicable. If, on the other hand, in killing, man unconsciously wants transcendence, then there is at least a way out: transcend the self; "kill" the self instead of others. (Wilber 1981b, 154)

But what of the rewards of this flirtation with death for the warrior?

The warrior's sacrifice returns him to the earth and to the victor's reward in death or inflates his hope for immortality through his survival. While war may have served evolutionary development by creating islands of cultural security, it has been too popular to be simply attributed to the development of culture. "For every one year of peace in mankind's history, there have been fourteen years of war" (ibid., 159).

A clue to the riddle of the warrior may lie in Hercules' death. He is restored to the good graces of Hera. The Great Mother receives him. Mythically, the warrior may be seen to choose the path of return, through physical death, to the realm of the Great Mother. He lays down his struggle for individual uniqueness, chooses the loyalty of his group, and offers himself to his ideals. The warrior goes home to the womb of the earth drenched in blood.

In my own inner exploration, I have found this ancient warrior and his fascination with the numinous qualities of blood and death. During the fall of 1982, the "warrior" awoke within me. In a series of inner meditations, I found myself immersed in the realm of blood, of death, and of bloodlust as a carnivorous animal. I came to know the "berserker" within my own shadow consciousness. During this time I reviewed many violent deaths in my mind, as if they were my own death or battles in which I had fought. I came to realize that my first taste was of the blood and amniotic fluids of birth— that earthly life is blood. In one very powerful meditation, I found myself weary with life, weary with struggle. The image came to me to take my life. A deep sadness and despair unfolded. I discovered that underneath the desire for death was the desire for release from effort. The weariness with my own egoic patterns of life as the hero-warrior of righteousness was evidencing as a desire for death. I realized that death is the *body's* way toward transcendence. The message of my body, in response to the desire for release from the boundaries of my own self, was death. What I most deeply longed for, however, was not death but *life* released from my self-imposed bondages. My journal entry of that day read:

> No more trying/efforting—exhausted with it. That is the part that wants to commit suicide, and it is very strong. It wants to be released. I want to be released from the effort, the struggle to find God. This body is, it seems, equipped primarily to find God through death— many violent deaths—some self-inflicted—mostly through battle. Now it is my task to help it learn to surrender to find the Presence everywhere.

Around this time, I received the following dream:

> I am getting to know a cadaver, playing with it, seeing how it moves.
> As I am working the hip joints Patti tells me to test out its sacral
> connection to the pelvis. If it is real loose, it is a good sign. I do so
> and lift up the back. The sacrum wiggles in all directions. That is the
> sign, she says, that he was a devotee. I ask, you mean, of Lakshmi or
> Kali? She says, Yes.

In the sequence of this meditation and dream, the archetypal images with which we have been working come together. Kali is the darkest of the Great Mother figures in mythic image, who is still worshiped in remote parts of India with animal sacrifice. But in the dream, the one asking for sacrifice can also become Lakshmi, the Hindu goddess of good fortune. Patti was a woman who in my childhood represented the higher feminine. She serves here as my guide to reconciliation with the dark feminine. The violent energies coming into my consciousness as warrior energy, as the receiving into myself of the numinous quality of violent death, can be received as pure energy to be used in whatever cause I choose, as shown in the capacity of the sacrum to move in all directions. That energy is the energy of external and internal violence. I found myself transmuting this energy into the sacred image of God as a refiner's fire, the column of fire devouring my old self-image and releasing me from the weariness with life that I was experiencing. My journal entry continued:

> I am becoming a burning bush, burning but not consumed. The
> person, the body, transformed by this encounter to burn with the
> energy but not be consumed by it. All the impurities being constantly
> consumed, yet the outward form continuing to remain—How
> amazing!

We have come to the point of transition, the midpoint between the hero-warrior and the hero-transcendent, the point at which they both converge, the encounter with God the Father, the terrifying power. The journal entry continues:

> I have been taught to fear God's coming in this way—"Who shall
> stand when He appeareth? For He is like a refiner's fire." And I have
> counterpoised with my brave little warrior—I can stand—I can be
> here unafraid. I will be David against both the Goliath of the unconscious and the God Almighty. But little David is tired and confused
> and at the same time aware of how much he has been programmed

to be afraid of this encounter, so even more confused. Only when all images drop am I at peace.

The hero-warrior contains extraordinary energy. He has learned to stand in the very midst of death unwaveringly. He has become, as did Hercules, a master of the world of death. Contained within our masculine bodies is this primal power, the power to face death directly and the power to transform earthly life through the blacksmith's fire of technological ingenuity. The hero-warrior *is* the capacity to undertake arduous tasks for the good of humanity.

Unfortunately, there is a great blindness in this aspect of the male soul. Within the quality of his allegiance lies both his gift to the world and ultimately his capacity for destruction of the world. That allegiance is to a culture or race and is often short of allegiance to all of humanity. The warrior has often served to advance the economic or political goals of one group over another. The hero-warrior needs another power to be complete. It is the power of the hero-transcendent to seek and find a transcendent vision with which to direct his powerful energies. When these two powers converge, we find the warrior for social justice, who appeared in the Old Testament and has come forth in dramatic form in Mahatma Gandhi and in Martin Luther King, Jr., in our time. Without tapping the hero-warrior's great reserve of energy and resolve, we will perhaps condemn our culture to stagnation. But without addressing his inherent violence and limited allegiances, we will find him reaping destruction.

To discover this needed balance, we will turn to examine the potentials and pitfalls of the hero-transcendent as envisioned in the West. We will then look for new images of male consciousness and the possibilities inherent in our time for the wholeness of the male soul, as he integrates both his warrior self and his spiritual fire.

Experiential Questions

1. The hero-warrior's world is a masculine world, with thousands of years of human history behind it. As you reflect on your life within masculine environments, what experiences of social structures, family, and work opportunities have influenced your understanding of manhood? Have your work relationships been primarily with men? What values and characteristics do you ascribe to the world of men?

2. What has your relationship been with the issue of authority? Has authority been granted to you by your culture, your work, your spouse? Have you had to create your own arena of authority? Has this authority been developed over the years in your life as it was in Hercules' growing powers? When did you achieve your full authority inwardly and outwardly, if you feel that you have done so? What skills and wisdoms contribute to your sense of authority? If you have not achieved this sense of authority, what issues do you need to address in order to do so?

3. How do your answers on questions one and two above correlate with your relationship with your father? Was he authoritarian or malleable in his role within the family, or a mixture of these styles? Did your father ask you to "earn" your right to authority or was it gradually given as you grew up?

4. Hercules' labors are performed alone, yet the history of the hunter-warrior was to be involved in groups of men for the purpose of achieving collective goals. What areas of your life mirror the solitary efforts of Hercules? In what areas do you seek companionship in working toward your goals?

5. A significant question was once posed to me: "Did you get to this point in your life primarily through effort or surrender?" The warrior knows the way of effort. Yet Hercules is cured of his fits of violence only when he surrenders in service to Omphale and is feminine for three years. Both modes are needed. Which is most natural for you? How would you cultivate the opposite mode now?

6. What is your experience of violence and/or aggression within yourself? Have you had experiences of your capacity for violence that alarm you? Are you able to convert your aggression into creative energy? Do you find that sports or other physical activity either as a participant or observer provide a release for aggressive energy? Do you feel that you need to cultivate more positive aggressive energy? How would you go about doing so?

7. How do you characterize your allegiances to family, race, culture, nation, God? Where does ultimate allegiance lie for you? Perhaps you disagree with the concluding assessment in this chapter of the hero-warrior's weaknesses in regard to allegiances. What allegiances are worth fighting and dying for in your opinion?

8. List the positive and negative aspects for yourself of being male in this time of history.

4

♦ ♦ ♦

THE HERO-TRANSCENDENT

As the Greek language was developing, a very early distinction was made between two words for our word *life*. These words are *bios* and *zoë*.

> [*Zoë*] "resounds" with the life of all living creatures. These are known in Greek as *zoön* (plural, *zoa*). The significance of *zoë* is life in general, without further characterization. When the word *bios* is uttered, something else resounds: the contours, as it were, the characteristic traits of a specified life, the outlines that distinguish one living thing from another. (Kerényi 1976, xxxiii)

This distinction goes to the core of the relationship between the hero-warrior and the hero-transcendent. The hero-warrior is concerned primarily with *bios*, with life within its given forms and contours. He works in the realm of technology and relationship with the visible forms of the world, whether these be the forms of civic life or the ability to track an animal. The hero-transcendent concerns himself primarily with *zoë*, life-as-such, with the underlying unity of life beyond its particular form. It will become clear that the hero-warrior also contains within himself characteristics of the hero-transcendent and that the hero-transcendent contains elements of the hero-warrior. However, the focus of each will be different. King Arthur contains transcendent elements within himself. But his relationship to both *bios* and *zoë* seem very different than the way St. Francis relates to *bios* and *zoë*. In this chapter we will focus on those, such as St. Francis, who have chosen to relate to life primarily through its quality of *zoë*.

By the hero-transcendent I mean to include a broad range of individual forms. The life of the hero-transcendent begins with the priest but is by no means limited to the priest. In the West, forms that this quest for *zoë* have taken include philosophy, art, music, drama, and theology, to name a few. For the purpose of this discussion, I will limit myself to the principal form of the hero-transcendent, the quest for truth as an inner experience. The roots of this hero-transcendent go to the beginnings of religious wonder. The mode of the hero-transcendent has included the shaman, witch doctor, and contemplative. What I will particularly examine is the Western approach to the inner life as a means of discovering the *zoë* residing within one's own being. *Zoë* is at the root of the Western relationship to its soul.

Plotinus used *zoë* in such a way that it could be conceived only as endless, unlike *bios*, which clearly has a time-bound existence. *Zoë* in the course of rebirths "moves on from one *bios* to another." When Plutarch or others, like the early Christians, wanted to speak of eternal life, they used the term *zoë*. And so the Christians did in their term *aionios zoë*, "eternal life." "*Zoë* does not admit of the experience of its own destruction: it is experienced without end, as infinite life. Herein it differs from all other experiences that come to us in *bios*, in finite life" (ibid., xxxv-xxxvi). The purpose of religion and philosophy is to bridge the two worlds. Greek religion brought the sphere of daily life and eternal life together through festivals "in which divine epiphanies are expected and striven for" (xxxvii).

The Mysteries of Dionysus

Dionysus and Hercules are the two sons of Zeus, who have human mothers. In the case of Dionysus, there are also stories of divine parentage, with Persephone as his mother. The myth containing the story of his human mother is quite intriguing. In this case, his mother is Semele, also identified as the "subterranean," as Chthonia, which links her to Persephone, the queen of the underworld. Semele's father was reported to be King Kadmos. At Thebes a burnt ruin that was in the sacred region of Demeter, the mother of Persephone, was reported to be Kadmos's palace (Kerényi 1951, 256). These connections of Semele with the chthonic element, and with Demeter, point to the very close relationship between Dionysus and the old forms of Great Mother worship. There are other connections as well. Dionysus is refered to as "'lord of the wild beasts'" (Kerényi 1976, 80). His adherents are predominantly women, although men can also fall under his spell. For these reasons an examination of the Dionysian mysteries seems most fruitful to our quest for the Western soul. Dionysus is the most direct link in the West to the ancient nature religions. Yet much of the imagery associated with him is brought into Christianity, thereby directly affecting contemporary spirituality.

The birth of Dionysus to Semele has many variations. But the essential point is that after Semele is with child by Zeus, Hera comes to her as a nurse and tells Semele to ask of Zeus that he appear to her in the same form that he comes to Hera on Mount Olympus. Semele elicites a promise from Zeus to fulfill one wish. Then when she asks to see him in his Olympian form, it is too late. Zeus must visit her in the form of lightning. She seeks to flee, but she is struck by the lightning and descends into the underworld. Zeus rescues the unborn Dionysus from her womb and sews him into his thigh until his time of gestation is completed (Kerényi 1951, 257). Dionysus is thus born both of woman and of man, and as we shall see, he is born yet a third time through dismemberment and resurrection. Dionysus is thus often called the "thrice-born." When he is born of Zeus, he is given into the care of nurses. Again, there are many versions of who these nurses are. The essential point is that, although he is born of Zeus, he is virtually in the exclusive companionship of women after his birth. Other myths point to a search by Dionysus for his mother, Semele, in the underworld, where he finds her and then takes her to immortality in heaven, as the goddess Thyone, "the ecstatically raging" (ibid., 259).

In this sequence, we may have unfolded for us the mysteries of Dionysian worship. The woman, Semele, is struck by lightning, an energy which plunges her deep into herself, into the underworld. Here is the theme of ego-death. Then through the ecstatic trance of the Dionysian mystery, she receives a direct perception of Dionysus, which brings transcendence. It is the saga of birth-death-rebirth. It also retains the central motif of the Great Mother worship, the eternal regeneration of the mother through a consort relationship with the son. For on his way into the underworld, Dionysus marks his way with a phallus made of fig-wood. And in one version of his birth, Semele is not impregnated in an ordinary liaison. Instead, Zeus gives her a potion of Dionysus's "heart" to drink. There is a play on words in these stories and in the Dionysian mysteries, in which "heart" and "fig-wood" stand for one another. Thus the element of the phallus becomes prominent in both his birth stories and the mysteries. In such worship, the phallus symbolically represents the life force. It is present to this day in the Hindu image of Shiva as the lingam (Campbell 1962, 170).

The worship of Dionysus took place both in public festivals and in secret mysteries. In each case, a frenzy of "madness" was evoked. In the most ancient forms of this divine frenzy, a wild animal or sometimes a human child was torn apart with bare hands and eaten. Kerényi (1976) suggests that this primal contact with animals was the origin of man's experience of *zoë*. In these rites, masks were worn to signify entering another reality. *Zoë* was experienced in the animal. The masks represented the hidden quality of *zoë*, of *zoë* as both near and yet also remote (80).

In another cycle of stories, it is Dionysus himself who is the dismembered one. Hera sends the Titans to destroy the infant Dionysus. He is cut to pieces, boiled, and eaten. But a goddess (Athene, Rhea, or Demeter, according to different sources) saves the heart, from which the child is reconstituted.

> The Epicurean Philodemus, a contemporary of Cicero, speaks of the three births of Dionysus, "the first from his mother, the second from the thigh, and the third when, after his dismemberment by the Titans, Rhea gathered together his limbs and he came to life again." Firmicus Maternus ends by adding that in Crete . . . the murder was commemorated by yearly rites, which repeated what "the child had done and suffered at the moment of his death": "in the depths of the forests, by the strange cries they utter, they feign the madness of a raging soul," giving it out that the crime was committed through madness, and "they tear a living bull with their teeth." (Eliade 1978, 369–70)

In this account the practices become clearer. *Zoë*, eternal life, is contacted through the ritualistic reenactment of the death, dismemberment, and resurrection of Dionysus. Furthermore, it is experienced in frenzied ecstatic "madness," in which the dismemberment is enacted. Why such practices should put one in direct communion with *zoë* seems fairly clear. There is no moment more alive than the moment of death. For anyone who has been present in the moment of death of another person or of an animal, it is clear that the life force, the *zoë*, the soul has departed. What once was animated is now still. *Bios* has ended. It has lost its contact with *zoë*. We might look to our carnivorous hunter ancestors for making this discovery.

In which case, with more domesticated life, contact with *zoë* was remembered in its primitive form in animal sacrifices. Contact with the life force now became ritualized, sometimes in the very chaotic form of the Dionysian mysteries. Within the further stories of Dionysus there is also a bridge to less vicious practices for encountering *zoë*.

That bridge lies in his association with wine and intoxication. Dionysus is the eternally renewing vine of the grape, which in midwinter lies dormant and seemingly dead, then sends forth tendrils of new growth, finally producing grapes. But more than the giver of the grape, he is also the giver of wine. *Zoë* is directly experienced in the process of fermentation. Even prior to the growing of grapes, the fermentation process was surrounded with mystery and religious festival in the production of mead, a fermented drink produced from honey and water (Kerényi 1976, chap. 2).

In the process of fermentation, humankind enters into a new relationship with nature. It is a relationship analogous to the metallurgic revolution in blacksmithing. Now in entering into relationship with nature through fermentation, humankind produces that which intoxicates, which gives an altered sense of perception. Through intoxication, humanity can enter into a previously unconscious realm. And as all other discoveries of mutual endeavor between humankind and nature, the invention of intoxicants carries its dangerous side. It is possible to become lost in one's intoxicating world and lose a grip on the world of ordinary reality.

The induced "mania" of the followers of Dionysus is seen by some scholars to be a state conducive to a direct perception of a divine epiphany. Such a direct experience of divine presence was the intent of the bacchic festivals. What the Greeks called *mania* was "a state in which man's vital powers are enhanced to the utmost, in which consciousness and the unconscious merge as in breakthrough" (Kerényi 1976, 133-34). Such is the state induced in the Dionysian mysteries.

As Kerényi discusses art works that have been discovered relating to the Dionysian mysteries, it is clear that in rituals of major initiation intoxication plays little if any role. He makes a distinction between the popular festivals in which wine played a major role, and the true initiation into the secret mysteries, which were much more concerned with a visionary perception of the god. There emerges here the distinction between exoteric religion in the public festivals, and esoteric religion, the practices that evoke a particular experience of the divine. In the rites of dismemberment and boiling or passing through fire, the Dionysian mysteries are very similar to the rites of initiation for shamans (Eliade 1978, 371).

Dionysus presents many faces to us. In his complexity, he was attractive to all classes of people, to ascetics as well as orgiastics. He brought the inducement of *mania* through intoxication and ecstatic *enthousiasmos* through contemplation (Eliade 1978, 372). Dionysus presents an experience of *zoë* to his followers, whether this experience be of a visionary nature in the secret mysteries or of a more visceral nature in the festivals of public intoxication. The same style of public and private festival continued throughout the history of Europe and still finds expression throughout the Christian world in the bacchanalian Mardi Gras preceding the inward focus of Lent.

This eruptive quality of life contrasts strongly to the sense of tragedy, evident in Hercules' story and throughout Greek literature. Something different manifests in Dionysus than in Prometheus or Sisyphus or Atlas, each with his unending task and burden. "Euphoria and intoxication in a way anticipate life in a beyond that does not resemble the gloomy Homeric otherworld" (Eliade 1978, 361). With Dionysian festivals, the whole Greek culture found itself involved in games, sports, and joy. Dionysus brings to the individual, bound by his isolated heroic quest for mastery of *bios*, the rediscovery of *zoë* beyond any success or failure in that quest. Dionysus creates space in public life for transcendence of the mundane, for *bios* to be reminded that it is grounded and sustained in *zoë*.

From Dionysus to Christ

Many of the themes present in Dionysian festival and myth find their way into the early Christian church. The Gospel of John, the most esoteric of the Gospels, utilizes many Dionysian images. In that Gospel, Jesus is introduced in his public ministry through the miracle at Cana of turning water into wine (John 2:1–11). The imagery of the vine plays a predominant role in the mystery of incorporation of the believer into Christ.

"I am the real vine, and my Father is the gardener. Every barren branch of mine he cuts away; and every fruiting branch he cleans, to

make it more fruitful still. You have already been cleansed by the
word that I spoke to you. Dwell in me, as I in you. No branch can
bear fruit by itself, but only if it remains united with the vine; no
more can you bear fruit, unless you remain united with me." (John
15:1–4, NEB)

Jesus continues, however, to define what it means to be united with
him, and through him with the Father. "'As the Father has loved
me, so I have loved you. Dwell in my love. If you heed my commands, you will dwell in my love, as I have heeded my Father's
commands and dwell in his love'" (John 15:9–10, NEB). He then
goes on to illustrate the quality of love of which he is speaking as
the willingness of a person to lay down his life for another. He has
invited his followers to dismemberment on behalf of the value of
love. Dismemberment for the receptivity of divine epiphany takes
on the vow of compassion as well. Revelries in and of themselves take
second place to the discovery of *zoë* as a wellspring of compassion.

The nature of the love required is elucidated by the love com-
mandment:

> "You have learned that they were told, 'Love your neighbour, hate
> your enemy.' But what I tell you is this: Love your enemies and pray
> for your persecutors; only so can you be children of your heavenly
> Father, who makes his sun rise on good and bad alike, and sends the
> rain on the honest and the dishonest. If you love only those who love
> you, what reward can you expect? . . . There must be no limit to
> your goodness, as your heavenly Father's goodness knows no bounds."
> (Matt. 5: 43–48, NEB)

The dismemberment required is now of one's own ego boundaries
and exclusive identification with one's group, nation, or clan. This
expansion of the nature of compassion was equally difficult for both
the Hebrew and the Gentile worlds to hear. We must remember
that Israel was an occupied nation when these words were uttered.
Jesus extends the notion of love within the Hebrew interpretation,
in which to love one's neighbor had the connotation of disdaining
one who was not of the Hebrew nation. Love had this connotation
in Greek culture as well. In the *Oresteia*, Aeschylus echoes the
popular ethic of retaliation, "Requite an enemy with evil." Jesus'
command radically alters this view of love, by commanding love even
of the enemy (Furnish 1972, 65–66).

In the Gospel of John, one cannot mystically "abide" in God the

Father without becoming involved in an active movement of love in one's relationships. Love is understood in the Gospel of John as *aionios zoë* coursing through the vine into the branches where it bears the fruit of deeds of active service. One cannot mystically "abide" in God without also actively serving the new ethic of universal love (ibid., 145). The Dionysian element here is the *active* nature of *zoë* as love. Such love, coursing through the veins of the vine and bringing it to renewal of life in springtime, is identified by Jesus as love expanding now to overcome the cultural barriers among the many clans and groups which the Roman Empire has brought together.

In this great teaching, we begin to find a resolution of the tremendous disruption to the Middle Eastern and Mediterranean worlds which we have identified as the epoch surrounding the Fall. When the massive geographic and sociopolitical upheavals disrupted the agrarian cultures around 1700 to 1400 B.C.E., exposure to cultures other than one's own began. The ethic that evolved in the face of such traumatic restructuring of interrelationships was: love within your group, but disdain or actively hate outside of it. If we may generalize at all from the history of Israel, such an ethic was most likely highly useful, because another clan or group was, like Israel, apt to want to annihilate you and take your lands. Now among the people of Israel, the "wine-bibber" Jesus calls for contact with the Father who is universal, the Father not merely of the people of Israel, but also the Father of all peoples, and whose *zoë* is universal love.

The intoxication of this contact with *zoë* is evidenced in the healings, forgivings, and other regenerations that take place both in Jesus' presence and in his postdeath presence in resurrected form or as the Holy Spirit. The quest of the Western hero-transcendent has been for this intimate relationship with *zoë* as energizing love within his own soul. Meister Eckhart (fourteenth century C.E.), one of the preeminent figures of this quest, wrote of the discovery of *zoë*:

> Saint John . . . calls [the Holy Spirit] an "intoxication" because of his quick emanation, for the Spirit flows just as completely into the soul as the soul empties itself in humility and expands itself to receive him. I am certain of this: if my soul were as ready and if God should find as much space in it as in the soul of our Lord Jesus Chirst, he would just as completely fill it with this "river." For the Holy Spirit

cannot keep from flowing into every place where he finds *space* and he flows just as extensively as the space he finds there. (Fox 1980, 363)

The Western quest has been to find *zoë* in the midst of *bios*. Jesus brought the message to turn that quest inward within oneself and within one's relational life: the kingdom of God is within/among you. Dwelling in the reign of God means finding the wellspring of universal love through which enmity among national and family groups could be overcome.

As the church developed after the crucifixion of Jesus and his resurrection appearances, the major issue that arose was whether or not the cult would remain within Judaism, requiring circumcision of men and the following of all the regulations of Jewish law. In answer to that dilemma, Peter is given a vision in which he is commanded by God to kill and eat "creatures of every kind, whatever walks or crawls or flies" (Acts 10:12, NEB). Many of these creatures were taboo to the Hebrews, so Peter responds with a refusal to obey. Three times the vision recurs. Soon thereafter, Cornelius, a Roman centurion, is instructed by a visionary appearance of an "angel of God" to send for Peter to come visit him. For Peter to come into his house is a violation of Jewish law (love within your clan but not outside of it). When Peter hears what Cornelius has to say, and reflects on his own vision of the cleanness of all creatures, Peter says: "'I now see how true it is that God has no favourites, but that in every nation the man who is godfearing and does what is right is acceptable to him'" (Acts 10:34–35, NEB). In the Letter to the Ephesians, the basic posture of the early church regarding this new understanding of the universal quality of love is stated eloquently:

Gentiles and Jews, he [Jesus] has made the two one, and in his own body of flesh and blood has broken down the enmity which stood like a dividing wall between them; for he annulled the [Jewish] law with its rules and regulations, so as to create out of the two a single new humanity in himself, thereby making peace. This was his purpose, to reconcile the two in a single body to God through the cross, on which he killed the enmity. (Eph. 2:14–16, NEB)

In Jesus' words and in the witness of early Christianity, there is a clear conviction that humanity is being called into a new relationship with God and with one another, a relationship of universal love through a deep and abiding mystical connection to *zoë* as love.

Fig. 10. Donatello, Crucifix. 1444 C.E. Padua, Sant 'Antonio.

The crucifixion holds the power of this transformation for which the hero-transcendent strives (Figure 10). Through this image, indellibly imprinted on the Western soul, the striving outward of ego-consciousness for authority over the earth and for conquest in the service of one's own limited aims is radically thwarted. Symbolically the Western dominance of the masculine principle demands a counterbalance. The crucifixion, with its demand that every ego-motivated quest be questioned, provides a powerful reminder of death, sacrifice, and surrender in Western life. In the crucifixion, the same paradox of the Dionysian mystery is presented in even

more compelling terms. Life springs from death. Ego must surrender. No more sacrifices are required to God to find this mystery,
for the ultimate sacrifice has been made. Through the pathway of
suffering, *zoë* as universal love is found.

While the principle of transformation of the individual into Christ
through participation in his crucifixion is preached in the early
church, there is considerable confusion as to what to do with the
ecstatic experience that sometimes accompanies this transformation.
The giving of the Holy Spirit on Pentecost evoked a phenomenon
of people witnessing to the resurrected Christ in languages other
than their own. Through this phenomenon, people from many na-
tionalities and groups heard this witness in their own tongues (Acts
2:7–13). At Pentecost, this new Spirit proclaimed a truth beyond
cultural barriers. However, when the phenomenon of speaking in
tongues begins to evidence as a part of ecstatic worship within the
church, it evokes controversy from the very beginning.

The Taming of Enthusiasm

In Paul's letters to the church at Corinth, it is clear that ecstatic
worship is taking place. There is a frenzied form of worship that
includes speaking in tongues, a direct communication between the
believer and God. There are also prophets, who are able to interpret
the tongues of others and decipher their messages for the general
congregation. Others are healers and teachers (1 Cor. 12:7–10). It is
also clear that the ecstatic enthusiasm of the new Christians reaches
proportions that are too excessive for Paul. Christ brings freedom.
A recurring theme throughout Paul's writings is to learn to live in
freedom in a way that breeds health rather than destructiveness. He
reports stories of sexual immorality, including the marriage of a
"man with his father's wife" (1 Cor. 5:1). He reports disorder in the
feast of the Lord's Supper, so that some eat and drink to excess
while others go hungry (1 Cor. 11:21). This is a far cry from communion wafers dispensed to the orderly lines of communicants of
our day! It seems that Dionysian-like practices are breaking out in
the early church in the name of Jesus, and Paul seeks to tame such
enthusiasm.

Paul's answer to these abuses and the many forms of community
dissent he reports is to seek love. It is in response to this particular

community, with its tremendous upheavals, that his most eloquent passage on love is given. And in this statement is a description of the emotional and ethical ramifications of the new form of universal love commanded by Christ.

> Love is patient; love is kind and envies no one. Love is never boast-ful, nor conceited, nor rude; never selfish, not quick to take offence. Love keeps no score of wrongs; does not gloat over [other's] sins, but delights in the truth. There is nothing love cannot face; there is no limit to its faith, its hope, and its endurance. Love will never come to an end. (1 Cor. 13:4–8a, NEB)

In the service of this form of love, Paul insists that the Corinthians bridle their ecstatic worship. The means he gives to tame their enthusiasm is the intellect. He calls reason into the domain of reli-gious frenzy. Ecstatic utterance without interpretation is ques-tioned. He concludes his admonitions with a description of the proper form of worship.

> To sum up, my friends: when you meet for worship, each of you contributes a hymn, some instruction, a revelation, an ecstatic utter-ance, or the interpretation of such an utterance. All of these must aim at one thing: to build up the church. . . . It is for prophets to control prophetic inspiration, for the God who inspires them is not a God of disorder but of peace.
>
> As in all congregations of God's people, women should not address the meeting. They have no license to speak, but should keep their place as the law directs. . . . It is a shocking thing that a woman should address the congregation. . . .
>
> In short, my friends, be eager to prophesy; do not forbid ecstatic utterance; but let all be done decently and in order. (1 Cor. 14:26–40, NEB)

A great deal is revealed between the lines of Paul's admonitions. The church at Corinth is clearly involved in a form of ecstatic wor-ship that to the onlooker might seem as frenzied as a Dionysian rite. We recall that the onlookers at the day of Pentecost accused many of the ecstatics of being drunk. Paul asks the worshipers to tame their enthusiasms with reason. He insists that they find a way to continue their ecstatic worship, but to give it order, so the meaning of the utterances is conveyed in a rational way to visitors and those not frenzied. We also note that the frenzy has clearly involved women as well as men, and that the women are henceforth forbidden to speak. Thus it is clear that in the new freedom of the Spirit, women have been equally sharing in all of these gifts of ecstasy until this time. Paul asserts the primacy of the intellect and its interpretation by males in the service of the newly discovered universal love. Henceforth in the West, those themes predominate. Western spirituality has never been far away from the effort to explain itself in philosophy, dogma, and theology. And there has been a great suppression of women's authority. Equally revealing in Paul's comments is the theme that ecstatic worship must give way to the service of the church. What upbuilds the church institutionally, what assists the church to communicate to the visitor, to the public at large, takes precedence over the enthusiasm of the individual believer. And unfortunately, Paul misses the obvious weakness of the intellect. It is his intellect that insists upon continuing the tradition of not allowing women to speak. It now seems clear from our vantage point that in the full inclusion of women, the Spirit was giving new directions to male-dominated structures.

The public life of the church bowed to the need to communicate through the intellect. It has systematically shunned the ecstatic, nonrational modalities of direct contact with *zoë*. Those seeking more eccentric modes for direct communication with God have continually moved away or been asked to leave the mainstream of Christian practice. And in this decision, we may also see evidence of the split between body and spirit that has dominated Western thought. For these forms of ecstatic worship clearly involved many manifestations of the body, including ecstatic utterance and healing practices. Paul insisted on the greater service of reason to the attainment of God. He was not alone, as we shall see. Reason becomes the handmaid of God, and the body with its passions becomes the distraction by which the demons would keep us from God. There are further reasons, which we will explore, for this deep distrust of the enthusiastic that looks so much like ancient orgiastic forms of worship. In the writing of Paul, it is clear that Western spirituality will take its cues from reason rather than from the ecstasy of the body.

St. Augustine's Vision

A clearer perspective on this issue begins to emerge through the writings of Augustine in the fifth century C.E. Augustine began writing *The City of God* in 413, three years after the first overthrow of Rome by barbarian invaders. That event sent a shock wave throughout the Roman world. In its aftermath, the ancients looked to Christianity as a scapegoat. They suggested that it was because of this new religion that Rome had fallen. Augustine reviews the history of Rome and points to the internal weaknesses within its own life. He particularly points to its roots in war and expansion of power, and its assumed right for global hegemony. Augustine is the preeminent hero-transcendent addressing the weaknesses of a civilization based on principles of the hero-warrior.

In his writings, he reviews many of the rites of the religious world of Rome. We see in him a man whose reason is fully awakened. He responds with moral revulsion to many of the practices he sees. He criticizes the dual life in Roman religion, in which the deepest philosophical truths are passed on in the private mysteries, while the public festivals contain unbridled obscenities. He points out the confusion apparent to his rational mind in the kind of rituals we have described as belonging to Dionysus. These rites included both public festivals of orgiastic drunkenness and private ceremonies in which the initiate came into an experience of the god's dismemberment and thereby came to a direct perception of zoë. What Augustine documents is the self-destruction of the Roman rituals, because they were a bridge between an older form of consciousness and the new emerging rationality. To the eyes of that new consciousness they seemed to be designed to keep humanity captive to unbridled passion, rather than to cause humanity to look to a new vision of the Eternal. Augustine's view was that these rites kept humanity in an infantile relationship to their gods, a relationship of fatalistic dependence on horoscopes and divinations. His most urgent issue, however, was the way in which these rituals and public games incited passions, which the same teachings then sought to bridle. He points out the bewildering moral climate of this transition time in human consciousness.

We see in his writing that the older forms of the myths, in which the gods and goddesses behaved with a great deal of passion and caprice, are exhibited in public rites, while the more evolved philosophical and ethical teachings are given in private. Augustine, together with Paul, calls these old gods demons.

Accordingly, in public, a bold impurity fills the ear of the people with noisy clamour; in private, a feigned chastity speaks in scarce audible whispers to a few: an open stage is provided for shameful things, but on the praiseworthy the curtain falls: grace hides, disgrace flaunts: a wicked deed draws an overflowing house, a virtuous speech finds scarce a hearer, as though purity were to be blushed at, impurity boasted of. Where else can such confusion reign, but in devils' temples? Where, but in the haunts of deceit? For the secret precepts are given as a sop to the virtuous, who are few in number; the wicked examples are exhibited to encourage the vicious, who are countless. (Augustine 1950, 69–70)

Lest we think this interpretation is only the viewpoint of a defensive exponent of an upstart religion among the Roman pantheon, we may remember the development of the Roman love for gladiatorial contests and festivals of massive bloodletting. Sometimes these games took on the quality of a myth, with the victim enacting an ancient theme. Martial and Tertullian attest to this practice. The following description by Martial clearly illustrates this form of public execution and enactment of the stories of the gods:

Even as Prometheus on the Scythian mountain
  fed with his growing breast the eternal bird,
Laureolus, not in mimic crucifixion,
  gave his bare flesh to a Caledonian bear.
His frame still lived when all the limbs were mangled,
  and all his body bore no trace of self.
At last his punishment was just: the scoundrel
  had stabbed his father's or his master's breast,
or in his wicked madness robbed a temple,
  or kindled Rome with sacrilegious [sic] fire.
He had surpassed the crimes of ancient fable,
  and now a fable was his punishment.
(Kiefer 1953, 97–98)

In this case, a public execution has been cast as a myth. There is an account of a similar execution portraying the myth of Orpheus (ibid., 98).

Seneca (4 B.C.E.-65 C.E.) worries over the morality of the arena: "Man is a thing which is sacred to mankind; but nowadays he is killed in play, for fun. It was once a sin to teach him how to inflict wounds or receive them; but now he is led out naked and defenceless and provides a sufficient show by his death" (ibid., 105). He has found the arena, with its emphasis on killing for entertainment, to become abhorent.

I have dwelled on this theme at some length, because it seems necessary to understand the milieu of passion that ruled Rome, in order to understand the countermovement against the passions that dominated early Christian spirituality. In his *Confessions* (vi, 8), Augustine cites the danger he saw in the arena from a psychological perspective. In that account, he describes a young man visiting Rome who went to the arena. At first he refused to go there, but was persuaded by friends.

> When he saw the blood, it was as though he had drunk a deep draught of savage passion. Instead of turning away, he fixed his eyes upon the scene and drank in all its frenzy, unaware of what he was doing. He revelled in the wickedness of the fighting and was drunk with the fascination of bloodshed. (1961, 122)

Augustine gives us quite a dazzling picture of the Roman world, with its festivals of public sexuality and Colosseum games of public bloodlust. No wonder he is so strong in advocating a religious structure that is also a structure for moral edification. He advocates religious practice whose public gatherings represent the highest moral ethic to which that religion aspires and shuns the dual structures of public debauchery and private moral teaching. With such an understanding of the world in which he lived, his passionate desire for people to find Christian practice and turn away from the "demons" is an expression of a new state of intellectual and moral alignment. His description of Christian worship gives us an image of decorum and moral edification. In their public worship, the sexes are separated, they are instructed in holy scripture and in righteousness.

> And though some enter who scoff at such precepts, all their petulance is either quenched by a sudden change, or is restrained through fear or shame. For no filthy and wicked action is there set forth to be gazed at or to be imitated; but either the precepts of the true God are recommended, His miracles narrated, His gifts praised, or His benefits implored. (1950, 72)

In this description of public worship, there is no hint of the ecstatic practices of Paul's Corinthians. Reason has triumphed. Augustine's form of public worship, with the exception of the separation of the sexes, might well pass for any mainstream Christian congregation in our day. The new spirituality searches for an alignment of morality with rational understanding, based in a re-presentation of the mystery of Christ's message of universal love.

Augustine's vision, in the midst of this upheaval of political, religious, and moral perspectives, gave birth to the doctrine of the two cities: the city of God and the earthly city. The first son of the earthly city was Cain, whom we have already met. And in his lineage, Augustine placed the world of passion, political action, and all temporal aims (ibid., 503). He makes much of the giving of a second son, Seth, to Adam and Eve after the murder of Abel by Cain. In this new son is given the image of the spiritual realities, beyond the concerns of the earthly realm (504). To Seth belongs the city of God. In Augustine's writings we find Western man discovering the distinction between operating from sense-bound motivation (*bios*) and operating from nonsensual motivations (*zoë*). To these two ways of being, he gave the names the earthly city and the city of God. With this clear division between the earthly city and the city of God, Augustine demarcates the structure of Western spirituality.

The Taming of the Passions

The history of Western spirituality might be read as an increasingly inward movement, an increasing interiority, the movement from external form to inward motivation. Liturgically, that movement shows itself in the sacrament of holy communion. In that ritual, there is a reenactment of the basic theme of sacrifice for atonement with God, which has its roots in prehistory. Millennia before Christ, there were sacrificial offerings made to the gods. We have previously discussed some of these roots. Such rituals sometimes involved human sacrifice, often animal sacrifice. In the Dionysian mysteries, through the ecstatic dismemberment of the live animal, the worshiper came into direct contact with *zoë*, the eternal quality of life, which sustains each unique and time-bound creature. Now, in Christ, "in the full, perfect and sufficient sacrifice for the sins of the whole world," the sacrificial relationship of humanity to God is ended, indeed reversed. It is now the man who is God, who dies. God makes the end of sacrifice through God's own self-sacrifice. Through this reenactment of that sacrifice in holy communion, the believer experiences *zoë* interiorly, as the core of love indwelling within his or her own limited existence as *bios*. It is a long route from tearing open a live animal in order to experience this contact with eternal life to experiencing the eternal dimension simply through the breaking of bread, sharing of wine, and remembrance of Christ's death and resurrection. So, on this public, liturgical level, we see a tremendous movement toward interior knowing, manifesting over the past three thousand years.

On the deepest levels of interiority, those levels in which there is no public liturgy at all, there has been a similar movement toward zoë. In the West, this has preeminently taken the form of monastic renunciation of the world: renunciation of Augustine's earthly city in order to find the city of God. The spirituality of the hero-transcendent, to which we are the heirs, felt it necessary to place the two cities in diametric opposition and to choose the city of God, leaving behind the earthly city.

A collection of writings called the *Philokalia* (Kadloubovsky and Palmer 1954) documents the struggles and teachings of Greek and Russian monastics in the Orthodox tradition. In the early writings, there is unanimous consent that in order to attain to God, one must first die to the ways of the flesh. Here, Christ crucified came to be identified with a crucifixion of all passions of the body. St. Isaac of Syria (c. 550) is typical in his admonitions. For him the admonition to leave the world in order to purify oneself meant leaving the "passions." "When we want to speak of passions collectively, we call them 'the world'; when we want to distinguish between them according to their different names, we call them passions. . . . the world is carnal life and minding of the flesh" (ibid., 187).

These early monastics sought a complete isolation from the excesses of the earthly city, which Augustine has catalogued for us. Not only that, but they sought an isolation from the organized structures of the church as it was developing. The quest of the hero-transcendent is the quest of the individual against the collective. He is a hero over against the collective claims of church and state. Herbert Workman, in *The Evolution of the Monastic Ideal*, states the fundamental act of individual protest that lay at the heart of the early Christian ascetic

His was the protest of the individual against the collectivism which tended, both in Church and State, by its institutions and foundations, to lose sight of his value. The monk, whether in the East or West, was the voice in the wilderness crying the lost truth of the worth of one soul. (1962, 23)

The model for the monastics was Jesus' experience in the wilderness, where he was tempted for forty days and nights. The same temptations that he faced figured prominently in the mythology of renunciation. The demons to be faced were lusts of the body, identified with Jesus' temptation to turn stones to bread; love of money and power in Jesus' temptation to receive all earthly kingdoms; and love of human glory in Jesus' temptation to make a public spectacle of himself. Herein are the roots of the later monastic ideals of chastity, poverty, and obedience. Abba Evagrius (d. 399) describes these three "demons" and sees them at the root of all difficulties. "In short, it is impossible for a man to fall under the power of any demon, unless he is first wounded by the three foremost" (Kadloubovsky and Palmer 1954, 117). In his writing, the demons no longer stand for the Roman pantheon, but for internal states of discontent. Their absence is a necessary prerequisite for a direct apprehension of God. A troubled mind is incapable of contemplating the divine. "Such luminosity (that is, untroubled thought of God) appears in the sovereign mind only on condition that thoughts turning among things during prayer are cut off" (118).

The writings of the *Philokalia* give us a clear picture of the methodology practiced by these early monks for attainment of inner quiet. A primary tool for subduing the passions is fasting. "An empty stomach makes of our ideas a desert land, silent and undisturbed by any turbulent thought" (ibid., 208). Silence and solitude are essential. "He who loves conversing with Christ, loves to be solitary. But he who loves to be among many is a friend of this world. If you love repentance, love silence" (207).

The reward for such efforts is a direct apprehension of God. When human knowledge is no longer chained to the realm of the senses and the conflicts of the passions, it can experience eternal realities directly.

> Then it can soar on wings to the realms of the incorporeal and sensory creatures; [it can] search out the spiritual mysteries, accessible to a fine and simple mind. Then the inner senses awake for spiritual doing, according to the order which will prevail in the immortal and incorruptible life; for then it has, as it were, undergone a spiritual resurrection even in this world. (194)

St. Maximus the Confessor (d. 655) speaks of the highest forms of prayer:

The highest state of pure prayer has two forms. One belongs to men of active life, the other to men of contemplative life. One is engendered in the soul by fear of God and good hope; the other by love of God and extreme purity. The sign of the first order is when a man collects his mind, freeing it of all worldly thoughts, and prays without distraction and disturbance, as if God Himself were present before him, as indeed He is. The sign of the second is when, in the very act of rising in prayer, the mind is ravished by the Divine boundless light and loses all sensation of itself or of any other creature, and is aware of Him alone, Who, through love, has produced in him this illumination. In this state, moved to understand words about God, he receives pure and luminous knowledge of Him. (ibid., 299–300)

Here, in the West, the most ephemeral of spiritual realms is discovered, the realm of direct experience of God, the realm of *zoë*. It is accessible to all monastics. A conversation between an advanced contemplative, Abba Joseph, and his disciple illustrates this potentiality. Lot, the disciple, approaches Abba Joseph with a question:

"Abba, as far as I can, I say my little office, I fast a little, I pray and meditate, I live in peace and as far as I can, I purify my thoughts. What else can I do?" Then the old man stood up and stretched his hands towards heaven. His fingers became like ten lamps of fire and he said to him, "If you will, you can become all flame." (A Monk of New Clairvaux 1979, 52)

The aim of spiritual life was to become transformed within this body. One of the primary gauges of this transformation process was the degree to which the passions ceased to trouble one. The underlying assumption is that one cannot attain the insights of the spiritual realm while also being involved in the body's passions. Passionlessness is a goal for spiritual growth. Abba Evagrius goes so far as to call passionlessness "the health of the soul" (Kadloubovsky and Palmer 1954, 107).

As the monastics strive toward passionlessness, they learn a great deal about the workings of the body, mind, and spirit. They become observers in great detail of those things that seem to feed the passions and those things that promote passionless tranquillity. In their careful observation of themselves, the monks seem to be in a laboratory experiment in human motivation. They themselves are the crucible of this experiment. What is awakened in the monk is an awareness of lower and higher centers of motivation; the higher motivations he calls thoughts of angels, the lower ones, thoughts of demons. Abba Evagrius describes the difference: "Angels seek to discover the nature of things and their spiritual meaning." He illustrates this with an inquiry into the nature of gold and its uses. "The thought of the demons does not know or understand this, but shamelessly suggests only the acquisition of physical gold, predicting the pleasure and glory to be had from it." The mind is neutral to all this, simply introducing the subject. How one deals with it will either stir up the lower passions or the quest for higher knowledge (ibid., 119).

A careful reading of these adventurous heroes in the transcendent realms suggests that men had arrived at a time of evolutionary development in which they needed to quiet the passions in order to understand their tendencies to be overcome by them and in order to listen to other qualities of the mind and spirit. In Abba Evagrius's reflection on the mind is the distinction between the analyzing, scientific mind, from which will come discoveries of the atomic and subatomic structure of gold, and the holding of the substance in mystic awe. These qualities of thought he attributes to angels, while the use of gold for personal wealth and adornment he attributes to demons. But he also makes the discovery that there is a simple human mind that presents objects without judgment. To be in this human thought mode is to be neither pulled by greed nor pushed by angelic curiosity. In this simple state of mind, one is receptive to direct apprehension of God.

For these adventurers into interiority, the warrior's battle for earthly hegemony became their own inner battle for tranquillity. St. Isaac of Syria uses such martial imagery to speak of the inner life. "This world is a contest and a field for contest. This time is the time of struggle. . . . There is only one law there—to watch and to resist" (ibid., 211–12). For St. Isaac, progress is defined both in moral terms and by the desire to "leave this body." "Shortcomings of your neighbour will cease to be worthy of attention in your eyes; you will long to leave this body with the same intensity of desire with which you long to be in the life to come" (ibid., 109). The goal of these early monastics was to come into such absorption with *zoë* that all distractions of the flesh ceased. Such inner tranquillity was also manifest in outward tranquillity, in the attitude of love toward all people. Any distraction from that aim was a demon to be addressed with the full range of interior fortitude and insight that the individual had already gained. The monk was to assume that such attention to interior motivations would be a very difficult battleground. The battle would be lifelong.

The Quest for Purity of Heart

The hero-transcendent of Western spirituality aims preeminently toward purity of heart. This is a perfection of emotions as well as of actions. The aim of such purity is a direct perception of God. The method is primarily the *via negativa*. Perhaps it is due to the influence of the crucifixion imagery that the West predominantly approaches God through a negation of the earthly city. Early questors for purity did so through the ascetic negation of passion. Whatever stirred the heart toward worldly desire was systematically avoided, evaded, or stamped out. Thomas à Kempis (fourteenth century C.E.) expressed his hope for fulfilment in this way:

> Lord, I have great need of Your grace, of Your great singular grace, before I arrive where no creature will hinder me [from] perfect contemplation of You. As long as any transitory thing holds me or rules within me, I cannot fly freely to You. He desires to fly without hindrance who says: Who shall give me wings like the dove, that I may fly into the bosom of my Saviour and into the place of His blessed wounds, and rest there. . . . Unless a man is clearly delivered from all love of creatures, he cannot fully attend to his Creator; this is the chief reason why there are so few contemplatives—that is to say, because there are so few who will willingly set themselves apart from the love of created things. (à Kempis 1976, 135–36)

The positive aspect of this form of spirituality is represented in its most eloquent form in an anonymous writing of medieval England (fourteenth century) entitled *The Cloud of Unknowing* (Johnston 1973). The passions have become much less awesome in this work. They are still distractions to the direct apprehension of God, but they are no longer treated as embattling demons. The author's suggestions for dealing with distracting thoughts now amount simply to letting them go and not engaging in quarreling with them. If they become too troublesome, he suggests simply giving in to them.

> When distracting thoughts annoy you try to pretend that you do not even notice their presence or that they have come between you and your God. Look beyond them—over their shoulder, as it were—as if

you were looking for something else, which of course you are. For beyond them, God is hidden in the dark *cloud of unknowing.* . . . There is another strategy you are welcome to try also. When you feel utterly exhausted from fighting your thoughts, say to yourself: "It is futile to contend with them any longer," and then fall down before them like a captive or coward. . . . This is, indeed, experiential humility. . . . Then like a father rescuing his small child from the jaws of wild swine or savage bears, [God] will stoop to you and gathering you in his arms, tenderly brush away your spiritual tears. (88–89)

The basic instructions for contemplative prayer involve "letting go." The author suggests the imagery of a *cloud of forgetting* below one and a *cloud of unknowing* above. Into the *cloud of forgetting* one lets go of all thoughts, all feelings, and all images. One beats upon the *cloud of unknowing* with one's desire to know God alone.

This is what you are to do: lift your heart up to the Lord, with a gentle stirring of love desiring him for his own sake and not for his gifts. Center all your attention and desire on him and let this be the sole concern of your mind and heart. Do all in your power to forget everything else, keeping your thoughts and desires free from involvement with any of God's creatures or their affairs whether in general or in particular. Perhaps this will seem like an irresponsible attitude, but I tell you, let them all be; pay no attention to them. (ibid., 48)

For this author, a discovery about the nature of the mind has been made, which henceforth distinguishes the hero-transcendent from the heroes of worldly wisdom. It is the limitation of the rational mind.

Try to understand this point. Rational creatures such as men and angels possess two principal faculties, a knowing power and a loving power. No one can fully comprehend the uncreated God with his knowledge; but each one, in a different way, can grasp him fully through love. Truly this is the unending miracle of love: that one loving person, through his love, can embrace God, whose being fills and transcends the entire creation. And this marvelous work of love goes on forever, for he whom we love is eternal. (ibid., 50)

Here we discover the flowering of Jesus' concept of universal love. Love transcends the barrier between the creation and the creator, between *bios* and *zoë*, between the earthly city and the city of God. The method for coming into this awareness is very simple.

So whenever you feel drawn by grace to the contemplative work and are determined to do it, simply raise your heart to God with a gentle stirring of love. Think only of God, the God who created you, redeemed you, and guided you to this work. Allow no other ideas about God to enter your mind. Yet even this is too much. A naked intent toward God, the desire for him alone, is enough.

If you want to gather all your desire into one simple word that the mind can easily retain, choose a short word rather than a long one. A one-syllable word such as "God" or "love" is best. But choose one that is meaningful to you. Then fix it in your mind so that it will remain there come what may. . . . Should some thought go on annoying you demanding to know what you are doing, answer with this one word alone. If your mind begins to intellectualize over the meaning and connotations of this little word, remind yourself that its value lies in its simplicity. Do this and I assure you these thoughts will vanish. Why? Because you have refused to develop them with arguing. (56)

Alignment with God has come to its simplest and most profound tranquillity through a tranquil contemplative practice, the gentle stirring of *zoë*, which is at the core of the human heart. As the Western monastic focused intensely on the love of God, the reconciliation between the earthly city and the city of God manifested.

Meister Eckhart also expressed this reconciliation between the two realms:

I am often asked if people can reach the point where time no longer hinders them and where neither diversity nor material goods hinder them any longer. Indeed this is so! Rather, they all point you toward God and toward this birth for which we find a similarity in lightning. It turns into itself whatever it strikes—be it a tree or an animal or a person. . . . Behold, this is what happens to all who are affected by this birth. They are quickly turned toward this birth in whatever is actual to them, no matter how coarse it might be. Yes, what formerly was a hindrance for you now is a benefit to you. Your countenance will be completely turned toward this birth. . . . Indeed, all things become for you nothing but God, for in all things you have your eye only on God. (Fox 1980, 243)

The Western hero-transcendent presents us with a somewhat baffling pattern. He flees from the world and his own passions ultimately to discover a realm of divine presence beyond passion or thought that turns out to be most accessible when he approaches it in love, love even of his own passions and thoughts. Here we begin to approach the theme of the following chapter, in which we will examine the reconciliation between the hero-warrior and hero-transcendent, which seems to be manifesting in the inner world of men in our time. The seeds of that reconciliation lie in the nature of the love proclaimed by Jesus, which leads eventually to a reconciliation not only among peoples of diverse cultures, but also to a reconciliation of the enmities within the inner kingdoms of each one of us.

Implications of the Via Negativa

Before leaving the Western hero-transcendent behind, however, let us draw a few of the implications that emerge from this survey of the origins of Western spirituality. A prominent theme has been the mistrust of human emotions. Another is a negative perception of the physical world. Another is the trust in mental process over physical awareness.

From a mythical standpoint, it is intriguing to note that the goddess mother of Dionysus is Persephone, queen of the underworld, while the divine mother of Christ becomes the queen of heaven. At the stage of evolutionary development in which Christianity comes to birth, humanity has discovered the direct perception of divine radiance. God has been discovered in a direct perception of *zoë*. St. John calls Jesus the light of the world. Paul is blinded by such a light. Eckhart speaks of God as lightning. Dante finds the radiance of heaven so blinding that he must have Beatrice as an intermediary. We are here in the realm of the most subtle and powerful forms of spiritual revelation. The author of *The Cloud of Unknowing* speaks of the healing power of contemplative love. "For the contemplative work of love by itself will eventually heal you of all the roots of sin" (Johnston 1973, 64). To dwell in the midst of this particular power is to be released from every lesser enmity. To dwell in this power is to dwell in the Father as Christ dwelled in the Father. In radiant love, the West has found its form of enlightenment.

In contrast to this upperworld radiance, Dionysus had offered passionately underworld ecstasy and affinity with the queen of interior depths. In their quest for light, Augustine and the early monastics rejected the physical ecstasy of the passions. They felt that the earthly city and its religious forms in the Roman pantheon maintained people in an enslavement to what Paul called the "lower nature." The heroes of transcendence were searching for a cleansing

from the powers of this physical nature and a release to direct contemplation of God. When they turned inward, they discovered a war
being waged between the lower and higher natures. St. Paul describes this war in a way that became normative for Christians:

> Anyone can see the kind of behaviour that belongs to the lower nature:
> fornication, impurity, and indecency; idolatry and sorcery; quarrels,
> a contentious temper, envy, fits of rage, selfish ambitions, dissensions,
> party intrigues, and jealousies; drinking bouts, orgies, and the like.
> I warn you, as I warned you before, that those who behave in such
> ways will never inherit the kingdom of God.
>
> But the harvest of the Spirit is love, joy, peace, patience, kindness,
> goodness, fidelity, gentleness, and self-control. There is no law dealing
> with such things as these. And those who belong to Christ Jesus have
> crucified the lower nature with its passions and desires. (Gal. 5:19–
> 25a, NEB)

As I have studied these early monastic writings, I have come to
a profound respect for the men and women who undertook this
path. They went into desert regions to live alone and to face their
inner worlds with a minimum of external guidance. If what we read
of the Roman world is at all true, they were indeed a passionate lot.
Our brief historical survey of some of the monastic writings indicates
a lessening of the theme of internal warfare over the centuries. *The
Cloud of Unknowing* is clearly written by a man less alienated from
and fearful of his inner thoughts and passions than Abba Evagrius,
whose goal was to "dry up the natural juices" (Kadloubovsky and
Palmer 1954, 107).

The monastic subservience of the passionate nature to the mental
nature has left its trail of difficulties. In some profound sense, it has
perhaps created the shadow of our contemporary age. The shadow
of radiant light is profound darkness. If the Western heroes of transcendence systematically eliminated fantasy because it whipped up
the passions, we are left with a diminished capacity for imagination.
If it sought the enlightenment of mental process over the awareness
of physical sensations we are the heirs of psychosomatic disorders.
It is intriguing to note that the first catalogued mental illnesses were
the "hysterias" of women who were seen by Freud. The last ritualistic esctasies were the "manias" of Dionysian women. That ecstatic
worship gave way to rational and moral religious teaching may well
be applauded. Its problem for us in our time, however, may be a
loss of socially honored forms for ecstasy and pentecostal enthusi-

asm. The need for tranquillity still abides. And the author of *The Cloud of Unknowing* gives clear advice to his readers about how to come into contemplative unity with God.

What is missing in the *via negativa*, however, and what seems to be reemerging of its own power is the capacity to journey into the underworld manifesting now concurrently with journeys into the heavenly world. If the journey toward awareness of the transcendent heroes of fifteen hundred to two thousand years ago involved a lessening of the powers of passion over them in order to awaken a more subtle energy, we may applaud their achievements. But we must look to our own inner guidance to perceive where the Spirit, which the New Testament calls the "Spirit of Truth" is drawing men in our day. As we will explore in the next chapter, I believe that we are drawn toward a new myth for this exploration: the myth of wholeness.

A twenty-eight-year-old seminary student reported the following dream and meditation:

> He dreamed of a very dark and primitive man, clearly a shadow figure of himself. He awoke quite disturbed with this image. In his morning meditation following the dream, he did not resist the shadowy man. Instead, he found that they came to embrace one another. As they embraced, they were swept up into radiant Light.

Here is a very different form of coming into the radiance of God than the way proclaimed either by the early monastics or by *The Cloud of Unknowing*. It is the way of soul in both its upperworld and underworld capacities. It is a way through which we explore all the dimensions of our inner world, the darkness as well as the light. It is a way that makes peace with the passions by embracing them.

The hero-transcendent calls us to go into the wilderness of our own solitude. In our era of history, in which so much attention is given to outward achievement, it is a very challenging task to be sent alone into ourselves. The hero-transcendent, however, challenges us to see that without periods of retreat from the world, we easily lose ourselves into the culture's current values and easily miss the deeper call to creative service that God may be issuing to us. We may consciously choose to undergo this period of profound inward searching or life may seem to thrust it upon us. The hero-transcendent challenges us to answer the call of the wilderness when it comes and to learn there to dwell in peace in our own solitude.

Experiential Questions

1. The hero-transcendent of history reminds us that men may be called upon to undergo a wilderness experience, a period of exile or isolation, a time of silence when interior values are deeply questioned. Have you had such a time of wilderness? Was it self-imposed or did it seem that other people or life itself imposed it upon you? Describe the gifts of this time. If you have not had such a time, write about your reactions to the possibility that it may come in the future.

2. How do you discern the highest good for yourself? Do you pray, meditate, reflect by writing in a journal, listen to your dreams, talk with others, read and reflect on the thoughts of others, or do you use some other form? How do you access the "reflective moment" for yourself in which you pause to consider alternatives in your daily decisions?

3. What has been your experience with the historical *via negativa* of Western culture as a negation of the body's energies and passions? How has this cultural bias against emotion, sexuality, and the body influenced you?

4. If you pray, do you find trustworthy methods for inner guidance in establishing your connection with the divine? What methods might you wish to explore?

5. Describe an experience of inner or outer reconciliation when "love" became alive and truly healed a situation.

6. Do you have a relationship with an inner figure of guidance such as Christ or the Blessed Virgin that you trust? Did you develop this relationship or did it seem to come to you?

5

♦ ♦ ♦

THE HERO-CREATIVE

A Serpent Coiled Around the Sun

Thus they came to a crossroads; then Zarathustra told them that he now wanted to walk alone, for he liked to walk alone. His disciples gave him as a farewell present a staff with a golden handle on which a serpent coiled around the sun. Zarathustra was delighted with the staff and leaned on it; then he spoke thus to his disciples . . . .

Remain faithful to the earth, my brothers, with the power of your virtue. Let your gift-giving love and your knowledge serve the meaning of the earth. Thus I beg and beseech you. Do not let them fly away from earthly things and beat with their wings against eternal walls. Alas, there has always been so much virtue that has flown away. Lead back to the earth the virtue that flew away, as I do—back to the body, back to life, that it may give the earth a meaning, a human meaning. . . .

Physician, help yourself: thus you help your patient too. Let this be his best help that he may behold with his eyes the man who heals himself.

There are a thousand paths that have never yet been trodden—a thousand healths and hidden isles of life. Even now, man and man's earth are unexhausted and undiscovered. . . .

Verily, the earth shall yet become a site of recovery. And even now a new fragrance surrounds it, bringing salvation—and a new hope. (Nietzsche 1954, 186–89)

Friedrich Nietzsche has given us a very powerful symbol for the new age of humanity: a golden sun surrounded by a serpent. In this symbol earth and heaven meet and merge into one purpose: the spiritual purpose of the individual toiling to upbuild earthly, material life.

From Pierre Teilhard de Chardin, a Jesuit priest, whose originating point in Christianity would seem to be very different than Nietzsche's, comes a similar sentiment:

> The resources we enjoy today, the powers and secrets of science we have discovered, cannot be absorbed by the narrow system of individual and national divisions which have so far served the leaders of the world. The age of nations is past. The task before us now, if we would not perish, is to shake off our ancient prejudices, and to build the earth. (Teilhard de Chardin 1969, 67)

> The organization of the human energy of the element, whatever its general methods may be, must culminate in forming at the heart of each element, the greatest possible amount of personality. (ibid., 76)

These visions of Nietzsche and Teilhard de Chardin each in their own way point toward the West's solution to the dilemmas of the soul. The solution involves a fulfillment of the individual. Through an isolated interior journey, the Western man or woman finds his or her own center of power, wisdom, authority, and personality. It is through the creativity of such individuals that new forms of collective life emerge. We will not depend upon the collective to provide the framework for individuality, rather we shall support the individual, and allow collective life to follow him or her in new forms of social life. There is, of course, great danger of hubris in such a path, danger that the individual will forget the collective, will align himself only with his own power and abuse his fellows. There is equal danger in the opposite position, that position in some sense represented in the dispassionate nature of the Buddha, whose claim is toward a unity beyond any individual uniqueness. The West, for better or worse, has chosen the way of individuation, of discovery of the unique center of divinity within body and personality, rather than the dispassionate release from all personality and uniqueness. The West, it seems, has chosen the individualistic nature of the early monastic's desert search apart from the collective but has rejected his *via negativa* in regard to the earthly city. Instead, the West has chosen to work out its individuation in a *via positiva*, in an alliance with the earthly city, a search for divinity within the material realm. Through the centuries, the monk's *via negativa* has been consistently balanced by those whom Bishop Bossuet called the philosophers of Satan, who have sought to unlock the riddles of nature on her own terms.

As you will recall, we have spoken of this spirituality of the middle way between earth and heaven, between matter and spirit, as the early manifestation of the hero-creative in the Hebrew tradition. There God summons individuals, such as Abraham, to undertake great tasks for the future upbuilding of the human race. God gives Jacob a new name, Israel, because he strives with God and man and prevails. God engenders into the fabric of the Western mind in the Hebrew tradition the expectation that the individual may be called and may serve a great cause through creative acts. In chapter 1 of this book, I have suggested that "this energy to struggle and create new worlds is the dynamic energy of the masculine principle" (7). What I want now to suggest is that this masculine spirit of adventure in the name of new creation comes to completion in our time in the call in the heart of every person to contribute to the upbuilding of the earth through human creativity. The blending of the spirituality of the hero-warrior, with its emphasis on mastery of earthly forms, and the spirituality of the hero-transcendent, with its emphasis on attentive listening to the ineffable will of God, comes to fruition in the willingness of each individual to listen for and heed the summons of God to put his or her whole life into the service of the renewal of the earth in our moment of time. This middle way between matter and spirit is the spirituality needed for the present era of the hero-creative.

A vision of positive reconciliation between earth and heaven is also present within early Christianity. It is the culminating vision of Western scripture given by John of Patmos in the book of Revelation:

Chapter Twenty-One
And I saw a new heaven and a new earth: for the first heaven and the first earth were passed away; and there was no more sea.
² And I John saw the holy city, new Jerusalem, coming down from God out of heaven, prepared as a bride adorned for her husband.
³And I heard a great voice out of heaven saying, Behold, the tabernacle of God is with [humankind], and he will dwell with them, and they shall be his people, and God himself shall be with them, and be their God. (Rev. 21: 1–3; Quispel 1979, 110)

The vision of John is of a *new* heaven and of a *new* earth. His vision is not simply of heaven. Rather, he presents the Western desire for the renewal of the earth, for the use of the new spiritual energy of the mind and spirit to create a new order of earthly life. "Behold, the tabernacle of God is with [humankind], and he dwells with them." The Western religious paradigm has been preeminently *In-*

carnation: God dwells in the midst of earthly life. In the very midst of *bios*, there resides *zoë*.

That discovery has now been made to the satisfaction of the Western scientific mind, as well as to the intuitive visionaries. The careful attention to *bios* has revealed that at the heart of every particular creation lies the mystery of *zoë*. In the contemporary translation of these two realities, *bios* is called "matter" and *zoë* is called "energy."

> Now relativity theory tells us that mass is nothing but a form of energy. Energy can not only take the various forms known in classical physics, but can also be locked up in the mass of an object. The amount of energy contained, for example, in a particle is equal to the particle's mass, m, times c², the square of the speed of light, thus:

$$E = mc^2$$

> Once it is seen to be a form of energy, mass is no longer required to be indestructible, but can be transformed into other forms of energy. (Capra 1975, 186–87)

A new heaven and a new earth become possible, indeed, eternally renewing themselves. Nothing is eternally fixed. God is dwelling in the center of creation. "There is no more sea." The sea is the primordial chaos with which the book of Genesis begins. Here, at the conclusion of scripture, the sea has passed away. The unconscious darkness between humanity and divinity has been bridged. *Zoë* need no longer be sought: it is eternally present. If we take Nietzsche's serpent to be matter and his sun to be energy, he too has presented us with this final resolution to the separation of humanity from God. "A serpent coiled around the sun" is the eternal dance between energy and matter.

> At the macroscopic level, [the] notion of substance is a useful approximation, but at the atomic level it no longer makes sense. Atoms consist of particles, and these particles are not made of any material stuff. When we observe them, we never see any substance; what we observe are dynamic patterns continually changing into one another—a continuous dance of energy. (Capra 1975, 188)

Nietzsche's symbol represents a profound shift from the earliest images of the serpent. And this change reflects the struggle of Western consciousness. In the earliest known representations of the serpent in human record, we find the serpent biting its tail, making an empty circle, or coiling around an egg. Consciousness is enmeshed in matter, in the struggle for survival. Humanity is wholly dependent upon the Great Mother. The sun is identified with the rising masculine consciousness, with the light of reason, with the Son of Righteousness, with the dispensation of reason, self-responsibility, and enlightenment. It is Zeus's thunderbolt and Eckhart's lightning that "turns into itself whatever it strikes" (Fox 1980, 243). It is the taming of fire for the release of humanity from captivity to nature. The sun is what the monastics so strenuously sought through a rejection of the serpent. They were heralds of the end of the "old earth and heaven." Now a new relationship between a new heaven and a new earth is revealed, a relationship of eternal cocreation. The golden apples which Hercules must find a way to steal (another image of the sun) are now found in the center of our own bodies. The enmity between the city of God and the earthly city is ended, because the city of God is energy dancing with the earthly city, which also is energy, but simply of a denser and more time-bound form. "Indeed, all things become for you nothing but God, for in all things you have your eye only on God" (Eckhart; ibid.).

In John of Patmos's vision, the new city is given from God. As humanity tastes and touches the eternal *zoë*, our perception of earthly life is changed.

[4]And God shall wipe away all tears from their eyes; and there shall be no more death, neither sorrow, nor crying, neither shall there be any more pain: for the former things are passsed away.
[5]And he that sat upon the throne said, Behold, I make all things new. And he said unto me, Write: for these words are true and faithful.
[6]And he said unto me, It is done. I am Alpha and Omega, the beginning and the end. I will give unto him that is athirst of the fountain of the water of life freely.
[7]He that overcometh shall inherit all things; and I will be his God, and he shall be my son.
(Rev. 21:4–7; Quispel 1979, 110–12)

Such authority over earthly matters and the creative renewal possible was depicted in the images of Christ in Glory, so prominent in medieval art and architecture (Figure 11). This figure shows the masculine energy of creation, tempered and humbled through the crucifixion, now able to assume full authority for the just administration of earth and heaven. I suggest that this image is a powerful one for the hero-creative. We are accustomed to meditating on Christ

Fig. 11. The Mission of the Apostles, 1120–32 C.E., tympanum of the
central portal of the narthex, La Madeleine, Vézelay.

crucified as an appropriate image of spiritual life. Can we be equally
comfortable meditating on Christ in authority, the Christ within us
in creative power dispensing new health to the world? The hero-
creative will find this center of authority within himself or herself
and pledge it to the discovery of the "thousand paths that have
never yet been trodden—a thousand healths and hidden isles of life"
(Nietzsche 1954, 189).

The new city of Jerusalem anticipates the spirituality of our time
with two other images, one having to do with God and the other

with humanity. In this crystal city, there is no temple: "for the Lord God Almighty and the Lamb are the temple of it" (21:22). There is no need for a special place of worship, because God is eternally present. Nor is there any longer any division with the earthly city, the city of the warriors and rulers of human society.

²⁴And the nations of them which are saved shall walk in the light of it; and the kings of the earth do bring their glory and honour into it.
²⁵And the gates of it shall not be shut at all by day: for there shall be no night there.
²⁶And they shall bring the glory and honour of the nations into it.
(Rev. 21:24–26; Quispel 1979, 114–16)

What is fascinating in this representation of the new age is that the kings of the earth bring *their* glory and honor into the new Jerusalem. If we take this imagery on the personal level, the ego brings its own fullness, the glory of its limited *bios* into the already glorious presence of *zoë*. The individual in his or her uniqueness is also honored. Ego is not destroyed, personality is not a thing to be lost in order to come into union with God; it instead brings its own glory.

Proceeding out of the throne of God is a pure river of water of life, "clear as crystal." From this water springs the "tree of life, which bore twelve manner of fruits, and yielded her fruit every month: and the leaves of the tree were for the healing of the nations" (Rev. 22:1–2; ibid., 116). From *zoë* proceeds the healing of the earth, even of the nations, its social structures, even the structures of the old earthly warriors. Here is the tree of life from which Adam and Eve were driven. Now they rediscover it in the midst of life itself. The earth, once the place of tortuous suffering, is revealed as health in the perpetual offering of new fruit month by month. "And there shall be no more curse" (22:3). Furthermore, there is no longer even any search for the sun, for righteousness, for truth, for God.

⁴And they shall see his face; and his name shall be in their foreheads.
⁵And there shall be no night there; and they need no candle, neither light of the sun; for the Lord God giveth them light: and they shall reign for ever and ever. (Rev. 22:4–5, ibid.)

In the age of the serpent coiled around the sun, God shall be accessible without the arduous asceticism of previous ages. God shall be found in body, mind, and spirit. No longer will body and spirit be pitted against one another. All energies, divine and earthly, join in the alleviation of earthly suffering.

Such imagery of wholeness comes into our contemporary lives in many ways. A very powerful vision of the new heaven and new earth was reported in the following meditation upon a dream. The dream occurred several years ago and has been a powerful motivation for the man since it arose. John was thirty-seven years old when he related this image to me. He spent the first part of his life in many business ventures and in a full exploration of his relational life. During the Vietnam War, he assisted a hill tribe to evacuate their threatened homeland and find new homes. In that venture, he strongly exhibited the skills of the warrior. He has since become a priest.

> Meditation (April 2, 1983)
> I recall my vivid dream of being on a hilltop and looking down into a valley and seeing 3 globes of light—transcendence—the size of basketballs, hovering over a ruin in the valley. As I gazed at the ruin and light which came from the ruin they moved toward me and entered me. I woke up feeling tranquil and calm.

The three golden globes are reminiscent of the golden apples that Hercules was sent to find. Now in John's dream, they have become a vision of light hovering over the ruins of the old earth. The mode of renewal this vision of divine light chooses is to enter John, to use the unique individuality of this man in its service. What the globes mean to John is illustrated in a prayer he wrote on the day of the meditation:

> My dwelling spirit abides in my being. This is my mansion, for all that exists in me is a glorious mansion of being. I feel the power of love and unity of [the] Trinity [of] body, mind, and spirit. Oh soul so vast and complicated [sent] into a process of existence that has seen and experienced so much; improve my divine nature and wholeness so that God and my fellow beings may truly experience my light.

John identifies the three globes of light as body, mind, and spirit, now in harmony. His task is to bring forth his own inner light in order to share that light with both his fellow beings and with God. He reminds us very much of the vision of the kings of the earth bringing their own glory and honor into the radiance of God. In the Western mode of transcendence, we become light bearers, each within our own centers of being.

The Crystalline Bed and the Holy Grail

The mythic bridge between the visions of radiance of the early monastics and our present male quest for wholeness lies in the stories of the quest for the Holy Grail. This myth arose spontaneously throughout Europe around 1100 to 1300 c.e. It coincided with the first crusade. And it coincided with the birth of romantic love in Europe. This is also the era of great devotion to the Blessed Virgin, as evidenced in popular spirituality and the building of great cathedrals in her honor. The feminine returned with power in this era, reengaging the masculine in new ways. Figure 12 shows this return, an image of Mary and child from the twelfth century. We see in this attention to the feminine a new sonship of the masculine. The male soul reencounters the feminine in all its dimensions in this era. From this new interaction with the feminine, the hero-creative emerges.

There are several versions of the Holy Grail, the most important of which are a French version by Chrétien de Troyes, a German version by Wolfram von Eschenbach, and the English version by Thomas Malory, *Morte d'Arthur* (Johnson 1974, 7–8). Joseph Campbell has dealt extensively with the various versions, as well as with companion stories such as Tristan and Isolt and Don Quixote in *The Masks of God IV: Creative Mythology* (1968b). Campbell's work is a monumental essay on the development of Western consciousness from the flowering of medieval Europe to the destruction of its vision depicted in Picasso's *Guernica*, which was painted in 1937. Two symbols predominate in Campbell's understanding of the movements of Western consciousness. One is the crystalline bed, and the other is the solitary knight on horseback.

Five "knights on horseback" dazzle Parsifal so that he thinks he has seen "five gods" (Johnson 1974, 90). Their armor, with scarlet and gold trappings, present to us the nobility of the warrior, whose task is "service to life through knightly deeds" (Campbell 1968b, 548). Campbell points out that by Cervantes's time, Don Quixote dwells in a wasteland. Knighthood has dissociated from honor. And in Picasso's *Guernica*, the horse is riderless. The era of the warrior has ended in the self-destruction prophesied in Hercules' death by his own weapons. In *Guernica*, humankind's unconscious raw

Fig. 12. Madonna and Child. Polychromed oak. Ile-de-France, twelfth century C.E. Museum of Fine Arts, Boston.

destructiveness has arisen and must be dealt with as such, without the cover of noble knighthood.

The other major symbol is the crystalline bed. Campbell finds in the Tristan story, as well as in Wolfram's version of the Holy Grail, that erotic love has come alive again in Europe. What is unique about this discovery is the virtual worship of the beloved. In the love grotto with its crystalline bed, the warrior finds meaning for his deeds of service. Gottfried, the poet of Tristan, illuminates its meaning:

> No one could wish to be anywhere else. And this I well know for I have been there. I, too, have tracked and pursued the wild birds and beasts in that wilderness, the deer and other game over many a wooded stream; and yet, having so given my time, I never made a real kill. My toils and pains gained no reward.
>
> I have found the lever and seen the latch of that cave, occasionally reached even the crystalline bed. In fact, I have danced up to it and back frequently and rather well; yet never have known rest upon it. (ibid., 66)

This is the same bed that caused Hercules' death, through the jealousies and deceptions of his marriage. Now it becomes the meeting place with one's beloved, and through the beloved, the meeting place with one's own true divinity. Whether this is a chaste bed, a bed of a man's own interiority, or a bed of mystical sexual discovery is a question that presents itself in the various versions of the Holy Grail and clearly was on the mind of monks and knights alike. For the Parsifal of Chrétien de Troyes, his liaison with his Blanche Fleur (White Flower) is chaste (Johnson 1974, 50). In Wolfram's version, Gawain, whom Campbell calls Parsifal's alter ego, has a veritable wrestling match with the crystalline bed. Gawain is the "model lover" and Parsifal, the "questing youth" (Campbell 1968b, 554).

These various versions point to the tensions between the old hero-warriors and heroes-transcendent. The tensions inherent in the doctrine of the Incarnation begin to manifest. If God truly is flesh, then through flesh one finds God. Yet the monastic route to God had been through a denial of the flesh. Campbell believes that Chrétien de Troyes's chaste version of the tale is the result of an effort to quell the growing return to nature. Chrétien de Troyes was a monk and his version translates the Grail symbols of earthly abundance into heavenly reward. In contrast, in Wolfram's version, a veritable cathedral is erected to enshrine the value of heterosexual love and the service of the knight to his beloved (ibid., 566). The dance thus begins between the serpent and the sun, the new earth and the new heaven.

I will not present a detailed discussion of Parsifal. I would refer the reader to Campbell's work (1968b) and to the book *He!* by Robert A. Johnson (1974). Johnson presents a Jungian interpretation of Chrétien de Troyes's version of the myth. Campbell has drawn to-

gether Wolfram's version, along with considerable commentary.
What I will do is present some of the basic images of the story, and
reflect upon contemporary issues for men, both in their similarities
and differences to the modes presented in the story.

The Holy Grail

We might first of all begin by inquiring into the goal of the quest,
the nature of the Grail. We have, in fact, already been doing so. I
would suggest that the Grail is the restoration of balance between
physical and spiritual life. It is the "serpent coiled around the sun."
The images of the Grail in various stories point to such an interpretation. In some versions, the Grail is a large bowl. Campbell presents a great deal of data supporting the theory that this bowl
represents not the chalice of holy communion, but the ceremonial
bowl of ancient mystery religions, with their representation of the
bounty of nature (Campbell 1968b, 429). Such a theme also surfaces
in the book of Revelation, when the tree of life is discovered and
the bounty of the earth is celebrated. Such bounty is a part of the
description of Parsifal's evening spent in the Grail castle. "As the
grail is passed about without a word, it gives each guest whatever
food he silently wishes for. He has only to wish and the grail produces the food or drink. A silver tray does likewise" (Johnson 1974,
53). That Chrétien de Troyes should also link the symbols of holy
communion to the Grail in his version is no surprise. For the symbols of Incarnation convey the vision of transformation within
earthly life and restoration of earthly life to abundance. "There is
some ceremony and then a procession comes in. A youth carries a
sword that drips blood constantly. Then a maiden comes bearing
the chalice, the Holy Grail itself. Another maiden comes bearing
the paten that was used at the Last Supper" (ibid.). In the midst of
the death-dealing sword, the symbols of holy communion bring the
feast of abundance.

In Wolfram's version, the Grail is the *stone*, the philosopher's
stone of the alchemical transformation of the individual within physical life. That stone takes us again to the imagery of the book of
Revelation and to its representation of the new heaven and new
earth. The new Jerusalem is built of precious stone, "the wall of it
was of jasper: and the city was pure gold, like unto clear glass" (Rev.
21:18, Quispel 1979, 114). "'By the power of that stone,' we read in
Wolfram, 'the phoenix burns and becomes ashes, but the ashes re-

store it speedily to life'" (Campbell 1968b, 430). The Grail in this version is the transformation possible in and through the material world, the vision of the eternal within the temporal. By gazing into the stone, one discovers the eternally recreating phoenix. In the science of our day, this path has come to completion. Through the careful observation of matter, its spiritual essence has now come into view. Matter gives way to energy, *bios* reveals its heart of *zoë*.

Wolfram's version presents a middle way between darkness and light. His intention is specified in his opening lines: "Blame and praise alike are inevitable for the man whose courage is undaunted, mixed of white and black as it must be, like a magpie's plumage" (ibid., 432). The name Parsifal or *perce à val*, means "pierce through the middle." His ideal is the middle way, the life of integrity in the midst of the ideals of heaven and the struggles of earth. Wolfram's ideal is stated at the end of his story: "'A life so lived . . . that God is not robbed of the soul through the body's guilt; yet can retain with honor the world's favor: that is a worthy work'" (Campbell 1968b, 432).

At the core of the quest is the hope of a resolution of the split between matter and spirit, a resolution of the issue of suffering, and a discovery of the individual-in-eternity through a visionary experience. The quest for the Grail is still very much at the heart of Western consciousness. Whether we take the way of leaving the world, dropping out of its time-bound structures to quest for a deeper visioning capability within ourselves, or whether we take the way of deep involvement within those structures, or whether we find ourselves alternating those ways, the quest is for the "second sight" that makes life in the flesh meaningful. For Western consciousness, it will be very difficult to satisfy those questions apart from the middle way. For the question Parsifal must ever keep before him is, "Whom does the Grail serve?" That question is the question of *zoë* understood as *active* love. It is the question posed in Jesus' understanding of universal love. To be conjoined to him in mystical union is also to concern oneself inevitably with one's social responsibilities. The flight from the world by the desert fathers finds its return in Martin Luther King, Jr.

In our present century, Nikos Kazantzakis has expressed this claim of responsibilities upon us in a grand vision of human aspiration in *The Saviors of God: Spiritual Exercises* (1960b). Kazantzakis is best known for his *Zorba the Greek* (1952), in which Zorba lives the spirit-in-the-flesh. Kazantzakis's figures, whether his Zorba, his Christ (*The Last Temptation of Christ*, 1960a), his *Saint Francis* (1962), or himself (*Report to Greco*, 1965), live and breathe the questions posed by "the serpent coiled around the sun" in a twentieth-century context. His own resolution to the quest is stated simply in his understanding of Greece. "In Greece a person confirms the fact that spirit is the continuation and flower of matter, and myth the simple, composite expression of the most positive reality" (Kazantzakis 1965, 148). Kazantzakis's spiritual exercises represent the union of the warrior and transcendent functions.

For Kazantzakis, individual man and woman hold the balance of the universe in their power, for each stands in a unique relationship to all the generations going before them and coming after them. And God is *dependent* upon our unique service. "Whom does the Grail serve?" It serves God. Katzanzakis's God is not the almighty ruler of the universe; he is instead the evolutionary thrust of the universe. And whether or not that thrust is successful always hangs in the balance.

> My God struggles on without certainty. Will he conquer? Will he be conquered? Nothing in the Universe is certain. He flings himself into uncertainty; he gambles all his destiny at every moment. . . . God is imperiled. He is not almighty, that we may cross our hands, waiting for certain victory. He is not all-holy, that we may wait trustingly for him to pity and to save us. . . . Within the province of our ephemeral flesh all of God is imperiled. He cannot be saved unless we save him with our own struggles; nor can we be saved unless he is saved. . . . It is not God who will save us—it is we who will save God, by battling, by creating, and by transmuting matter into spirit. . . . Life is a crusade in the service of God. Whether we wished to or not, we set out as crusaders to free—not the Holy Sepulchre—but that God buried in matter and in our souls. . . . My God and I are horsemen galloping in the burning sun or under drizzling rain. Pale, starving, but unsubdued, we ride and converse. (ibid., 104–7)

Kazantzakis enables us to find in our own momentary quest for meaning the universal service to which Western man has been called since the age of the Hebrew prophets. We discover the Grail when we live as valiant warriors in the midst of the struggles that life is constantly thrusting upon us.

> As soon as you were born, a new possibility was born with you, a free heartbeat stormed through the great sunless heart of your race. . . .

Whether you would or not, you brought a new rhythm, a new desire, a new idea, a fresh sorrow. Whether you would or not, you enriched your ancestral body. . . . Where are you going? How shall you confront life and death, virtue and fear? All the race takes refuge in your breast; it asks questions there and lies waiting in agony. . . . You have a great responsibility. You do not govern now only your own small, insignificant existence. You are a throw of the dice on which, for a moment, the entire fate of your race is gambled. (ibid., 71–72)

"Where are you going?" is the question of egoic man released from the smallness of concern simply with his own pain, with his own loss of comfort from his ancestral roots or his mother or the Great Mother. Alone, he faces his darkness by standing strong and asking the question, "How may my life serve the universe?" Nietzsche answers:

Let your spirit and your virtue serve the sense of the earth, my brothers; and let the value of all things be posited newly by you. For that shall you be fighters! For that shall you be creators!
. . . There are a thousand paths that have never yet been trodden— a thousand healths and hidden isles of life. Even now, man and man's earth are unexhausted and undiscovered. (Nietzsche 1954, 189)

The male soul has thrived on service, prehistoric service to his clan in the gathering and hunting of food, service to his state, service to the ideals and ideas of his gods. What we discover in the image of the Holy Grail is the necessity for our positing a form of service to *both zoë* and *bios*, to both God and earth, to both spirit and flesh. And therein, in the "thousand healths" as yet undiscovered, we will find our own transformative Grail.

The Fisher King and the Innocent Fool

The context for our quest for the Holy Grail is set eternally in the passing of power from one generation to the next. In the stories of the Holy Grail, this passage of power is represented in the relationship between the Fisher King, who is old and very ill, and Parsifal, sometimes known in his youthful innocence as a Fool. The wounding of the Fisher King has happened many years ago. He came across a camp, empty, but with a salmon roasting over a fire. He reached for a piece of the salmon but badly burned himself in the process. He was also reported to be wounded in his thigh or testicles (Johnson 1974, 9, 13). Due to the wounds to his generative powers, his whole kingdom suffers. He is the aging king, so well known in the ancient Great Mother traditions. He has fulfilled his life, and now his kingdom is barren because the time has come for his removal. Even so, he continues to preside over the Holy Grail and its gift of earthly plenty. Yet he cannot heal himself. We have met the King Fisher before. He is Kronos. He is the aging order, the older generation, the older law, whom Kazantzakis calls upon us to surpass in the service of the evolutionary God.

What is awaited is a new youth. Parsifal's name means "innocent fool" (ibid., 17). In his innocence, he finds his way quite by accident into the Fisher King's palace, where he receives a vision of the bounty of the Holy Grail. The vision happens while he is quite young. And he neglects to notice the old man's suffering. He neglects to ask the fateful question, "Whom does the Grail serve?" The result of his negligence is that he awakes from sleep the next morning and has lost the Grail castle. The Fisher King must have Parsifal ask the question or he cannot be healed.

In this impasse, we discover the ancient intergenerational feud between men in the passing of power. The fathers, the Fisher Kings, have learned the secret of the Grail, the need for meaningful service. Yet they may become so enmeshed in their own forms for expressing that service, so identified with their own structural forms, that they are allowing the kingdom to crumble around them. They know fresh ideas, Nietzsche's fresh modes of "health," are needed for the good of all, but they hold on to the reins of power, in the desperate hope that the *right* young Parsifal will come along, in whom they can entrust *their* kingdom, failing to remember that the kingdom belongs to the evolutionary God. And Parsifal, for his part, is so dazzled, so astonished by the obvious power and suffering of the father as well as his abundance, that he forgets to ask the question of service. He is not yet ready to understand that this old man is his brother in service to a greater cause.

The obvious question this part of the story raises for men of our time is whether or not we are willing to enter into relationships of brotherhood and communal sharing with one another in the service of the earth, regardless of our age differences or positions of status and wealth. Without this sense of camaraderie in service we remain stuck, as we seem to have been throughout the masculine era, in jockeying for power with one another, forgetting to ask the essential questions, "Whom do we serve? Where are we going?"

The relationship between the Fisher King and Parsifal offers a hope that, for the sake of the ailing kingdoms, we can find means of mutual service with one another. When, after many years and much suffering himself, Parsifal reenters the Grail castle, he asks the question, and the Fisher King is healed. It may be that the Fisher King himself needs to be reminded by Parsifal's question. Now that his own security has been won, he may have lost touch with the deeper purpose of his life. And he may have grown insensitive to the youthful enthusiasm of others posing the question. The Kronos in each of us has the tendency to "eat" our children, to devour the younger generation in order to maintain our own hard-fought security. We must cultivate an openness to the youthful Parsifal to find release from our infirmities.

And so, very much hangs on the relationship between fathers and sons, whether these be the fathers and sons of the flesh or fathers and sons of any nation. Why do the fathers continue to send their sons to war, their eighteen-year-old Parsifals? Perhaps to avoid the confrontation with their own woundedness. Kazantzakis calls upon the Fisher Kings to release their world to the Parsifals:

> Your first duty, in completing your service to your race, is to feel within you all your ancestors. Your second duty is to throw light on their onrush and to continue their work. Your third duty is to pass on to your son the great mandate to surpass you. . . . Agony within you! Someone is fighting to escape you, to tear himself away from your flesh, to be freed of you. A seed in your loins, a seed in your brains, does not want to remain with you any more. It cannot be contained in your entrails any longer; it fights for freedom. . . . And you, the father, rejoice to hear the contemptuous voice of your child. "All, all for my son!" you shout. "I am nothing. I am the Ape, he is the Man. I am the Man, he is the Son of Man!" (1960b, 74–75)

I have played out the scene of taking power from my father in a visionary experience. In that vision, I found myself acting out one of the ancient rituals of the destruction of the old king by the new king. In my own psychic world, it was necessary to wrest my own power from him. After coming into my own power in this inner imagery, I then discovered the exquisite joy of being simply his equal. In a subsequent vision, I found myself alongside him. *We were two charioteers equal in power, flying toward the sun!*

As we learn to share both our youthful innocence and vitality and our ancient Fisher King woundedness, a possibility of a new intimacy between men arises. It is this new relationship which Birkin looked to find with Gerald in D. H. Lawrence's *Women in Love* (1976). Their story is the story of innocence and woundedness shared, but not yet fully shared. In Gerald's death, Birkin is left with an emptiness which a woman cannot fill. "Birkin remembered how once Gerald had clutched his hand with a warm, momentaneous grip of final love. For one second—then let go again, let go forever" (471). After the burial of Gerald, Birkin and his wife, Ursula, are talking:

> "Did you need Gerald?" she asked one evening.
> "Yes," he said.
> "Aren't I enough for you?" she asked.
> "No," he said. "You are enough for me, as far as a woman is concerned. You are all women to me. But I wanted a man friend, as eternal as you and I are eternal."
> "Why aren't I enough?" she said. "You are enough for me. I don't want anybody else but you. Why isn't it the same with you?"
> "Having you, I can live all my life without anybody else, any other sheer intimacy. But to make it complete, really happy, I wanted eternal union with a man too: another kind of love," he said. (472–73)

The Red Knight and the Fight: Another Kind of Love

Is there another love? A special kind of love between men, between fathers and sons, between brothers, between friends and colleagues? I believe there is. There is a potential for a "robust" love, a rowdiness, whether of locker-room banter or of hard-fought contests through which respect is mutually won. With another man, one's full power and authority are called into question, and thereby called forth. Kazantzakis speaks of his comrade relationship with God:

> Our love for each other is rough and ready, we sit at the same table, we drink the same wine in this low tavern of life. . . . As we clink our glasses, swords clash and resound, loves and hates spring up. We get drunk, visions of slaughter ascend before our eyes, cities crumble and fall in our brains, and though we are both wounded and screaming with pain, we plunder a huge Palace. (1960b, 108)

Let us hope that less and less in the fortune of humanity men must be called upon to be wielders of destruction in warfare. Yet let us not lose the special quality of comradeship that the history of warriorship has given to men. It is the ability to stand as comrades in the face of the destructuring and restructuring of the world, and even there to find a lust for life.

When Gerald and Birkin encounter one another during a particularly difficult time for each of them, they turn to a physical wrestling match to release their energies. Birkin pays Gerald a surprise visit.

"What were you doing?" [Birkin] asked.

"I? Nothing. I'm in a bad way just now, everything's on edge, and I can neither work nor play. I don't know whether it's a sign of old age, I'm sure."

"You mean you are bored?"

"Bored, I don't know. I can't apply myself. And I feel the devil is either very present inside me or dead."

Birkin glanced up and looked in his eyes.

"You should try hitting something," he said.

Gerald smiled.

"Perhaps," he said. "So long as it was something worth hitting."

. . .

"Some old Johnny says there are three cures for *ennui*, sleep, drink, and travel," said Birkin.

"All cold eggs," said Gerald. "In sleep, you dream, in drink you curse, and in travel you yell at a porter. No, work and love are the two. When you're not at work you should be in love."

. . .

"There's a third one even to your two," said Birkin. "Work, love, and fighting. You forget the fight."

"I suppose I do," said Gerald. "Did you ever do any boxing—?"

(Lawrence 1976, 259–60)

After a bit more sparring to set up the match, they strip and go to it. It is at the conclusion of their fight that they exchange the handclasp to which Birkin refers when Gerald has died. In the fight, they discover their love.

In the stories of the Holy Grail, the fight is assumed. The ethic of the knight is to involve himself in such contests on behalf of worthy causes. When young Parsifal encounters his first knight, an awesome one called the Red Knight, he has no difficulty whatsoever overcoming him. Parsifal has a natural agility on the battlefield. His father and brother before him have gone into battle. Because of their departures, his mother had withheld Parsifal from any contact with knightly life. Even so, his prowess is strong. In the contest with the Red Knight, Parsifal both contacts his own aggressive nature and gains mastery over aggression. The relationship of Parsifal with his mother on this point is well stated in the myth. It is the mother's function to protect and to preserve the children. And she will especially seek to protect the boy even from his own aggressiveness. There comes a time, however, when he must prove himself in the other dimension, the world of men. In that arena, she cannot help him. He must find his own power and aggressive capabilities. In his interpretation of the meaning of Parsifal's contest with the Red Knight, Johnson states that it is essential for a boy both to contact his aggressive power and to become master over it. Every boy must learn how to "master this violent side of himself and integrate that terrible masculine power for aggression into his conscious personality." Then he can use his power to overcome obstacles and achieve goals (1974, 27–28).

Recently, poet Robert Bly has been suggesting that men have lost contact with this natural aggressiveness exhibited by Parsifal. In the effort of the last few decades to cultivate their feminine side, something has been missing. Bly identifies what he calls the "soft male," who is not interested in harming life and yet who seems not to have much energy to give to life. "They are life-preserving, but not exactly life-giving" (Bly 1990, 3).

In his work with young men, Bly has discovered a flood of grief and discontent, not only because of the remoteness of their fathers (the inability of the Fisher Kings to share their woundedness!) but also because of the trouble within their marriages or relationships. They had learned receptiveness and empathy and were able to give it to their partners, but at the point that they were called upon to give direction to their lives or relationship, they were unable to do so. "In every relationship something *fierce* is needed once in a while: both the man and the woman need to have it. But at the point when it was needed, often the young man came up short." Bly cites an episode in the *Odyssey* where Hermes instructs Odysseus to lift his sword when approaching a maternal figure. Bly believes the soft male has confused showing the sword with using it. He has submerged his own power rather than learning to use it wisely (ibid., 4).

How well I remember the time my sword flashed in my marriage. It was one of those turning points where my own vow to my life's purpose was at stake. I flashed in deep anger to stake out the territory of my life beyond which I would not accept intrusion of any other person, not even the one with whom I am most intimate. And well I remember when my wife flashed her sword at me, similarly carving out her path. What is interesting now, several years after each event, is that we each in our own time embraced the path the other was suggesting. In the moment, however, there was a need for fierceness.

This ability to know one's aggression, but not be dominated by it, seems to be surfacing as a major issue for men in our time. Statistics regarding murder find most such acts to be momentary outbursts toward someone known to the killer. Often alcohol is involved (Lunde 1975). How as men can we not lose our energy in a wimpish denial of power and at the same time delve into our aggressiveness and free its energy? The path of service to a restlessly creative God requires such fortitude and strength, a tamed and positively directed aggression. In our era, when men often do not train for life with the aggressive practice of the knight or even the athlete, what assistance for this contest of life can we glean from the tales of the Holy Grail?

From Wolfram's account comes a mighty battle fought by two knights of equal strength, Parsifal and Feirefiz. Feirefiz is from an Islamic land. The things that inspire him to battle are the passionate love of women and fine gems. Parsifal's inspiration is from faithfulness to God and his own children. In their meeting together, they are "born of their father." "The lion, they say, is born dead from its dam; its father's roar gives it life: these two men had been born of battle din" (Campbell 1968b, 558). They fight so fiercely and so evenly matched that finally they must call off their match. Feirefiz is mottled colored, a mixture of black and white, as his life represents the mixed life of the worldly man. When the two, each almost dead, stop their fight, they realize they are lost brothers. The scene is reminiscent of another scene in which, in a similar battle, Parsifal and Gawain meet their match in each other. We are in the same arena that Birkin and Gerald enter when they wrestle to exhaustion. An intimacy is born for men in this contest with one another in equal strength. And although Jacob and Esau did not physically fight each other, emotionally Jacob wrestled with Esau throughout his life, until he was willing to meet him again face to face.

There is another form of love! It is the love born of two men of equal power. Whether this birth happens with another physically, as with the legendary knights, or with one's wits and prowess in business ventures, or with one's spiritual development in the relationship between teacher and student, to find a match for oneself is to be born of the lion's roar! How I value the men with whom I have met my match and thereby been able to grow through assertion! How difficult it is to cherish these struggles when one is in the midst of them! This necessity of finding our deeper masculine aggressiveness has been discussed at length by Robert Bly in *Iron John: A Book about Men* (1990), where he asserts that it must be found uniquely within the male experience.

To return to our knightly metaphor, it is necessary for a man to learn to use his "sword." We cannot come to wholeness by repressing our aggressiveness, although it is important to learn to contain our aggressiveness. We come to wholeness by making friends with our instinctual depths and claiming our power. Through this discovery of deep masculine power we find the ability for "forceful action undertaken, not with cruelty, but with resolve" (Bly 1990, 8). In this venture, we can also find sources of assertive power within spiritual traditions. It is only our watered-down versions that present Jesus as a kind young man, or present the benign aspect of the Buddha without Manjushri, the sword-bearer, or present enlightenment without Shiva, the destroyer. In fact, our spirituality suffers when we do not claim the powerful images of such fierce masculine powers. During a period of intense purification in my own spiritual pilgrimage, a time when everything externally and internally was in flux, I dreamed of Shiva, the Hindu god of creation and destruction. At the time of the dream I knew nothing about Shiva. When I discovered that he simultaneously destroyed and created the universe, I found the spiritual symbol for my life experience. But I was not fully content until I rediscovered the fierce Christ in the beginning pages of the book of Revelation. Here, coming on clouds, with eyes of fire and wielding the sword of truth, was the transformer I needed to assist me in this time of fierce change. At this juncture, let us assert that what we learn from the Grail stories about male assertion is that this power, to be simultaneously direct, forceful, and compassionate, is something that men may learn most directly from their relationships with one another. And let us assert that there is a place in the symbolic realm for masculine forms of God, holding a fierce and demanding sword to our lives.

The Crystalline Bed

Let us hesitate no longer to announce that the sensual passions and mysteries are equally sacred with the spiritual mysteries and passions.

Who would deny it any more? The only thing unbearable is the degradation, the prostitution of the living mysteries in us. Let man only approach his own self with a deep respect, even reverence for all that the creative soul, the God-mystery within us, puts forth. Then we shall all be sound and free. (Lawrence 1976, vii)

These words, written in 1919, appear in the foreword to D. H. Lawrence's *Women in Love*. They speak clearly the ethos of the new age of the "serpent coiled around the sun." No longer will the sensual passions be removed from the realm of spiritual development. But side by side these two parts of ourselves, what Lawrence calls "desire" and "aspiration," will guide us (vii). These two routes to truth are already present in Wolfram's account of the Grail.

There are many tones to love in Wolfram's story, and yet another in Chrétien de Troyes's version. Each sheds some light on the relationship between men and women. I shall certainly not attempt anything like an exhaustive statement on this immense subject. Rather, I shall let the images of the story simply convey their own metaphorical meanings to us.

The most passionate of the stories, although all are passionate in their own way, is that of Gawain. Gawain is seen by Campbell to be the man of the world, whose way to the Grail is through sensual passion. We find his most difficult ordeal to be the confrontation with the *marvel bed*. In Gawain's story, this experience is the equivalent of Parsifal's visit to the Grail castle. The people in the castle of marvels are held under a spell. Gawain, and all knights who enter the castle, have the right to undergo the test of the marvel bed. The usual result of those who do attempt it is death. Or a knight is allowed to leave with honor and not attempt it. If he conquers the bed, all the castle and its ladies, knights, and lands are his. That the bed is understood as a way of transformation is made clear by the description of its antechamber, "a great hall with a ceiling of many hues, like a peacock's tail" (Campbell 1968b, 494). The peacock is a clearly recognized Christian symbol of regenerative transformation, recognized in Augustine's writings (ibid., 501–3). Wolfram's intent is clear. Here, in the life of passionate sensuality is also the way of transformation.

The description of the bed makes it clear that we are, in fact, in the midst of the erotic manifestation of the new Jerusalem, which John of Patmos describes: "her light was like unto a stone most precious, even like a jasper stone, clear as cyrstal" (Rev. 21:11; Quispel 1979, 112). The marvel bed "stood on four wheels made of rubies on a floor of jasper, chrysolite, and sard, so smooth that he could scarcely keep his feet" (Campbell 1968b, 494–95). The bed is Gawain's philosopher's stone and new Jerusalem. We are also reminded of Ezekiel's vision of God enthroned upon the chariot (Ezek. 1:4–28). Here, in the chariot bed of man and woman, God is realized. "Every time he tried to touch it, the bed darted from his reach . . . 'like a reluctant bride in rebellion against the embrace being forced upon her'" (Campbell 1968b, 495). In this symbol is a powerful statement of man taking responsibility for his sexuality. Gawain faces the bed alone, as much a test as any other of the tests we have encountered in our survey of heroic adventures. His *via positiva* in regard to the erotic is fraught with as many difficulties as the monk's *via negativa*. Finally, he makes a leap of faith worthy of any existentialist. When he leaps upon the bed, it dashes about the room uncontrollably. Gawain is barely able to hold on. At last its fierce thrashing subsides. But then he is attacked on all sides by slings and arrows. A village churl dressed in fish skin attacks with a club. A lion rushes toward him with such violence that his claw sticks in Gawain's shield, and the arm remains attached after Gawain cuts it off. In one final lunge, the lion attacks him, but Gawain's sword goes through its chest. Gawain swoons unconscious from the battle (ibid., 495).

In this ordeal, Gawain has encountered the vengeance of the old feminine order. Both the fish and the lion are symbols of the power of the goddess (ibid.). In encountering this feminine vengeance, Gawain also awakens his deep male aggression. The churl is the most rustic of men in Gawain's world. He is a reptilianlike figure in his fish skins. Gawain bears away with him the lion's arm, reminiscent of Hercules' bearing off the skin of the Nemean lion. Gawain reminds us that a very direct route to the deep masculine of which Bly speaks is through our sexuality. Just as the deep masculine power can be awakened and integrated through contests with other men, it can be awakened and integrated in our contest with our sexuality.

When Gawain comes to, he is all gentleman. He apologizes to the maiden who is attending his wounds and begs her forgiveness for being found in such a state. "'If you would not mention it to anyone,' he said, 'I would be grateful'" (ibid.). His knightly dignity is offended at being found unconscious. Yet he entrusts himself to the maiden and asks her discretion in seeing him so vulnerable. The mighty knight is also very tender and vulnerable, and willingly shows this side to his lover when safety is assured.

All of this, as well as other tests, have been undertaken by Gawain in order to win the love of the lady of his heart, Lady Orgeluse. When he completes his last test, he approaches her to embrace her. At first, she resists being embraced in "iron arms." However, she soon yields herself to Gawain (ibid., 500). As they journey toward the castle, she weeps and explains that Gawain is not the first she has sent on these tests. The Fisher King was sent and thereby received his wounds. So, in a sudden surprise, Parsifal's story and Gawain's come together. The Fisher King is not wounded in Wolfram's story by the theft of the salmon, which Chrétien de Troyes interprets as the curse borne by every soul, the sweet taste of eternal life from which we are cut off by earthly life. The Fisher King has been wounded by his erotic love for Lady Orgeluse. Yet, are these two wounds so very different? In both cases, the wounding involves a separation from nature, from the feminine matrix, and from the bounty of the earth. Gawain succeeds through an awakening of the power of his loins, while the Fisher King remains wounded and defeated in his loins. The question men face in their relationship with the erotic could not be stated more eloquently: Will we be able to come into our own power in relationship to the feminine?

Parsifal's relationship with women seems less central than it is to Gawain. For Gawain, the relationship is the central motivation of his life. For Parsifal, the discovery of the Grail is central. Parsifal's relationship with the feminine, however, has much to teach us. In Chrétien de Troyes's version, his relationship with his love is chaste. "They lay in an embrace, head to head, shoulder to shoulder, hip to hip, knee to knee, toe to toe. But it is a chaste night; they are as brother and sister" (Johnson 1974, 32).

What men can learn from this version of the story is the value of coming into brother-sister relationships with women. We have discussed the healing that can be accomplished between older and younger men, between the Fisher Kings and the young Parsifals, when we realize together that our lives serve a higher evolutionary purpose which requires us to come into brotherhood. There is also a role for men and women as brothers and sisters in the service of God and humanity. To realize that there is a potentially chaste yet intimate relationship available to us among many, many people gives tremendous freedom to our relational life. Parsifal and Blanche

Fleur represent the epitome of spiritual intimacy. They lie with their bodies in full contact, yet they refrain from sexual embrace. I have known many women in this way—not literally lying so, but emotionally and spiritually matching our energies *in pursuit of the Grail*. That Grail quest with my sister comrades has taken many forms: political action and community service, as well psychotherapeutic and spiritual exploration. One of the first of these for me involved a woman twenty years my senior, with whom I have engaged in many community-oriented projects. Such relationships everywhere abound for men if we will open ourselves to them. In fact, the changing face of the workplace in our time now demands that men learn a new coequality with women.

I would go so far as to suggest that this chaste intimacy is the relationship with our mothers which is also ultimately healing to us. Within the womb and in infancy, we have shared the most intimate of spiritual and physical bonds with our mothers. Our mothers, for many of us, have been our first love. We then broke away to find our Lady Orgeluse. Now, in adulthood, we may choose to return to our mothers and cultivate the relationship of the chaste intimacy of brother with sister.

In Wolfram's version, Parsifal is wed. His relationship is very dear to him. After many years of wandering in a wasteland following his first error in the Grail castle, he visits with a hermit and describes his life. "'My greatest grief,' said Parzival, 'is for the Grail; my second grief for my wife. I yearn for them both'" (Campbell 1968b, 469). In this description by Parsifal of his priorities, we find a type of man who is very different from Gawain. For Gawain, relationship is the fulfillment of his life. He would never say he misses the Grail more than his Lady Orgeluse. Lady Orgeluse is his Grail. For Parsifal, however, there is an interior quest apart from relationship which must be satisfied. Perhaps Gawain is the model extravert, finding his life's meaning primarily in relationship, while Parsifal is the model introvert, finding his life's meaning in an interior quest. The hope or despair of these stories (however one wishes to read them) is that all characters seem to suffer equally, regardless of their primary focus.

In this version of the tale, Parsifal weds Condwiramurs. After Parsifal rescues her from a marriage of custom being forced upon her, they themselves wed. For the first three nights of their marriage, they lay as did Parsifal and Blanche Fleur. On the third night

they embrace sexually as well. "'And it was only after this consumma-
tion of the marriage purely in soul and spirit that the bond, already
recognized as confirmed, was substantiated through extension to the
physical estate'" (Campbell 1968b, 443). Although such notions may
seem hopelessly old-fashioned, they remind us that more is joined
together in our unions than genitals. Parsifal and Condwiramurs
represent the search for the Grail in their relationship as surely as
Lady Orgeluse and Gawain do in theirs. Parsifal and Condwiramurs
seek a union of their total beings and are able to experience this
unity whether or not their sexual expression is involved. Their style
gives a corrective to the perhaps overzealous expression of sexuality
in casual relationships in our time. It is not unusual to discover
young people today rather lost in the maze of instant sexuality, who
are seeking for models of other styles of relationship. Parsifal and
Condwiramurs represent such a middle road between the marriage
of convenience and custom on the one hand and a relationship of
sheer passion on the other (ibid., 441). They remind us of the spiritual and emotional bonding that customs of courtship were intended
to encourage.

What Parsifal may lack in passion, he more than makes up in
loyalty. When he is battling for his life with Feirefiz, it is the memory
of Condwiramurs and their two children that inspires him. Feirefiz's
battle cry is "Thabronit," which is where his *amor*, Queen Se-
cundille, resides. In battle, when Parsifal seems to be faltering,
Condwiramurs's memory comes to him. It is their life together with
their children that gives him strength to endure (ibid., 558). This
love, the love of loyalty to wife and children, is also a powerful form
of a man's love, indeed, for many of us, the primary motivation of
our lives.

Heart's Sorrow and the Loathly Damsel

The many faces of love are represented in yet two more of special
interest, hardly romantic, however. These are in Parsifal's mother,
whose name means "Heart's Sorrow," and in the Loathly Damsel. We
have already read how Parsifal's mother kept the knowledge of
knightly ways from him, because her husband and other son had gone
off adventuring. I do not want say much about Heart's Sorrow. I will
leave that to the many researchers into the feminine of our present
time. She is perhaps wiser than she is given credit for being. After all,
there is a knowing that comes from being the bearer of children, from

staying in place long enough to incubate an embryo and nourish a child to maturity, that may rightly question all this venturing forth in questing. Heart's Sorrow may well wonder at all this going forth in the name of love, when love already resides in the hearth of Parsifal's home with Condwiramurs. What we do know is that Parsifal is deeply grieved when he hears of his mother's death. In a tragic encounter during his adventures, he discovers that his mother has died of grief. Something here deeply touches me about my relationship with my mother, who also sometimes grieves my adventuring, as Heart's Sorrow grieved for Parsifal. The man's youthful zest for the Grail and for his own fulfillment necessarily means moving out and away from his mother, involving a second cutting of the umbilical cord as he enters adulthood. Somehow it must be done and somehow will most likely be painful for both son and mother. Yet, cut we must. Someday, the deepest reconciliation can come, as it does for Parsifal, when we fully realize our own responsibility as sons for both the clinging and the cutting. And perhaps, if we are very fortunate, we will reconcile fully with our mother and enter into a new level of relationship, as indicated before, that more closely resembles adult brother and sister, a kind of comradeship of the spirit.

As for the Loathly Damsel, she has one of the very best parts of the story. She is the one who confronts Parsifal when as a youth he has made it to the round table as a victorious knight. She is the one who knows the difficulties Parsifal has left behind him, the trail of botched attempts at heroics and the broken hearts. She accuses him and casts him into a solitary journey. After he has wandered for five more years, she again comes to him, this time to invite him once more to visit the Grail castle and attain its prize. She might be seen as the truth and bitterness of life earned through existential suffering. She could be seen as the call of the unconscious plunging Parsifal deep into his own inner journey, into his solitariness. She may manifest in many forms. Johnson interprets her as the "destroying, spoiling quality in a man at about middle age. Suddenly the savor has gone out of everything" (1974, 75–76). "She had a great nose, like a dog; two protruding boar's tusks, and eyebrows braided to the ribbon of her hair, bear's ears, a hairy face, and in her hand a whip with ruby grip, but fingernails like a lion's claws and hands charming as a monkey's" (Campbell 1968b, 450). It is clear that she bears many of the forms of the old Great Mother era—the boar, the bear, and the lion.

That she is the terrible feminine rather than a masculine form is interesting. Perhaps she is the ghost of Heart's Sorrow, now come to serve as strenuous guide. Perhaps she is the residue of the denial of the soul in Western culture. In that case, she is the earthy, chthonic depths of a man coming to haunt him at his prime of success and awaken him with nightmares (perhaps of snakes as she did in my case or with one of the other dark feminine images). I suggest that she is the soul, awakening us from too easy a slumber in the world of achievement. She comes to invite us to a wholeness that involves a deep interior journey. That she is loathly represents the denial and the abuse she has felt for centuries. The monastics have fought her visions of earthly pleasure and the warriors have fought to rid themselves of her compassion. In our time, when she calls us, may we respond as faithfully as Parsifal and set off on the interior quest for our own souls.

I would like to conclude this chapter with a story, pointing to the possibility of such a renewed connection of the male soul to the earth and to the feminine. The myth arose spontaneously in a man, age thirty-eight, during a visualization exercise in which he was asked to see two parts of himself coming toward him on a path. I think the story is not simply reflective of his own personal issues but represents an updating of the Grail story for our times. I have entitled it:

The Grail King and the Pregnant Lady

I set off up Mill Creek Road, which is bordered on one side by a small creek and on the other by steep green hills on which black cattle were grazing. Trees line the road, which winds uphill—quite steeply. It was a beautiful sunny day. I knew the path I wanted to follow, it was off to the left about three miles up. From the road it looked as if originally a road might have existed there, a sort of a T-junction, but no—too many old trees, too narrow, only a short distance from the road, and the creek to cross. But I was going up there—to where? It got steep and narrow and windy very quickly, but soon, light up above—the light indicating the top of the hill. I looked again. There were two figures up there waiting.

As I got closer, I made them out. One was a kingly figure, crown on his head, ornamented and embroidered clothes, and a two-edged sword in his left hand, held up in front of him at waist height. The other was a naked woman. She was beautiful. She was young, with long dark hair and deep brown eyes. She was pregnant, with full breasts. Who was she? The kingly person was older, bearded. I began to talk to him first.

We went off together to his kingdom and to his castle. It was built on the top of a hill. The castle was built on the very top with the city cascading down the sides of the mountain clinging to and hugging the sides. The streets were narrow—cobblestone—with beautiful but tiny, quaint houses lining each side. I kept wondering, "Why the sword? What is it for?" I didn't ask.

The king took me round to visit some of the people in their houses. We met quite a few older people. They all loved their king because he was so good to them. Whenever they were in trouble for food or clothing, they could go to him and he would help them. In fact, he was helping some every day. They liked him, too, because he visited them often, and because he was fair. He heard their tales and woes and was always just.

Then we went up to the castle to explore. He had no wife and family, but the castle was neat and clean and warm, because he had many courtiers and helpers. They were not to be seen because they were busy. The king delegated his authority to them and so they administered the kingdom—but always according to his fairness and kindness—the king was fair to them too.

I wondered still about the sword. Was it a sign of his role in his army as leader of the fighting force which defended the kingdom? That thought made me sad. I didn't want him to be a soldier, a killer. Was it a sign of his role as final judge and arbiter in disputes and arguments? Was it the sword of the courts which could cut off peoples' heads? I'm not sure whether I asked. I was afraid of the truth, that the king might be a severe judge and even a tyrant underneath. He wouldn't say or give a hint, or I wouldn't ask. But I was looking for any clue because I realized that the king was also me—myself in control and in charge. I didn't really want to be a tyrannical king. What was behind those doors?—but I wasn't allowed to see.

So I thought about the woman and decided to go off and visit her. She took me to her house and there to my surprise I found many children. Whose children were they? I didn't know and wasn't told, but they were all happy and loved the woman. She was their mother.

She cared for them with love. The woman was very easy to be with, but did not talk much to me.

I wondered about the child in the womb: Who was the father? Was it the king?

It was time to deliver her new child. There was no difficulty—an easy delivery, a beautiful baby and a very happy and healthy mother. But yes, it was the child of the king. He came, when he heard, to see his baby. He had no wife of his own.

The people in the kingdom found out and a problem arose, as some would no longer accept this man, who had a mistress and a bastard child, as their king. They wanted to get rid of him. Others loved him dearly and understood that he was king, but also human. He had failed, but so what. He was good and loving and fair. I embraced the king. I loved him even after such a short time.

Then bells began to toll. Was there a wedding? No, too somber and slow for that. Was there a funeral? Yes. Whose funeral? The king's? No. The woman dying after giving birth? No! Whose? I found out then that it was the death of the kingdom. It had split and died, because of the rejection by some people of their king. They couldn't approve nor ever accept and forgive his involvement with the woman as his mistress. I wanted to embrace him again. I felt sad, very sad.

The king loved the woman and went to visit her and all the children. While he was there, the children decided to go out and talk to all those who rejected the king. Off they went. I did too. The split kingdom caused sadness all around. There was no peace and happiness. There was fighting and jealousy and accusations. "Come back!" shouted and pleaded the children. "Forgive the king, accept him as human. He is a loving and good and just person. You all know that."

Many were touched by the children's pleas, and saw in them the goodness of the woman and the goodness of the king. Many came back.

Then there was real joy. Not only was there a healed kingdom, but there was also a wedding. The king married the woman. She was now his queen, dressed in finery with colored robes and ornament.

I had left them and was running up into the hills with much joy in my heart. I was so happy. But there was still the question in my heart—why the sword?

In this story, the "Grail King" is renewed by his relationship of intimacy, honesty, and fatherhood. His kingdom, split over issues of moral propriety, is restored by the innocence of children. The story offers hope that men may learn to enter more deeply into relationships of intimacy and truth with others and with themselves. Crises may be occasions for the discovery of our souls. Social structures, encrusted with custom, may momentarily suffer during this period of individual renewal. But they too may be restored to vitality through the innocence and love the children offer.

The Grail quest material presents a kaleidoscopic view of the issues facing contemporary men. The material shows us the many facets of the male soul with which we must come into relationship. It is not sufficient to be a man of material life, the legacy of the warrior, whose role is to become proficient in the ways of *bios*, life in its material form. The knights of the Grail quest learned to utilize their considerable skill as warriors on behalf of their greater community and on behalf of an awakened loving heart. Nor will the Grail material allow us a purely spiritual journey divorced from the concerns of earthly life. *Zoë* is not to be found in a renunciation of the concerns of family and community. Instead, the stories of the Grail point us toward incarnational living: the discovery of the Spirit in the midst of the world, and the reverence for all forms of life discovered through meaningful service to the earth.

And "why the sword?" Perhaps it can now begin to be relegated to symbol as it seems to be in the new story. It can become the symbol of personal authority and service fully awakened. The power of the sword is available, but there is little need for killing.

In the Grail stories, Western man is coming of age. He finds that he must truly encounter the multidimensional self he has become. He must learn to unravel the mystery of his relationship with woman in its many forms. He learns to encounter man also in a variety of forms. And he learns in all of these relationships that he is actually questing for his own visionary expression of God. He is learning to find his unique mission in life and to express it. In the midst of these numerous quests, he heals his own male soul.

Let us turn now to the possibility within each of us for discovering the male soul, the eternal and primordial source of life, hope, passion, and action.

Experiential Questions

1. The hero-creative challenges us toward positive relationships in many arenas. List significant women in your life and then describe the relationship. Is it a work relationship, an intimate relationship, a relationship of friendship and support, a relationship of intellectual or spiritual cocreation? Perhaps it has yet another type of character. Observe your capacity for a wide range of relationships with women. Have you made peace with "woman?" What areas are not yet at peace?

2. List significant men in your life and then describe the relationship. Is it a work relationship, a relationship of friendship and support, a relationship of intellectual or spiritual cocreation? Does it have a quality of intimacy? Perhaps it has yet another type of character. Observe your capacity for a wide range of relationships with men. Have you made peace with "man?" What areas are not yet at peace?

3. What is God or life circumstance asking you to create in the world during the current era of your life? What are the internal and external resources you bring to this process? How does this task differ from previous tasks you have undertaken in the past? How is it similar?

4. Have you made peace with God? Are you at peace with the realities of life as you experience them in this world? Do you experience God as masculine or feminine, as both masculine and feminine, as a spirit or energy beyond gender? Perhaps you experience God in many different ways. Refer to your answer to question four in chapter 3. Is there a relationship between the way you experience God and your life experience of effort and surrender?

5. If you are a parent, describe each child by name, age, and a few characteristics. How has each individually awakened you to creativity within yourself? What new aspects of your own personality have each called forth in you? How have you contributed to each of them to assist them to become the hero-creative for their lifetimes?

6

◆ ◆ ◆

THE HEALING QUEST

As we have journeyed into the Western male soul, we have found many gifts and problems. I have tried to present a balanced picture of the legacies of the hero-warrior, the hero-transcendent, and the hero-creative. As we look at the total picture presented by these three forms of male experience, we find a legacy with many problems. There are problems for men in the area of aggression and violence and in a limited understanding of the potential for creative relationships with women in many diverse roles. We also find the male struggling with his relationships with men in authority and with men as coequals in companionship. We find a negative view of emotions and the human passions. We find men in many ways cut off from others, as well as from their sources of both passionate energy and compassionate vision. However, we would be very unfair to this journey to leave it with this pessimistic view. As we draw this healing journey into the male soul to a conclusion, I will focus on the gifts that we can bring forward into our time from this last three thousand years of the male experience. We will again also speak of the problem areas in light of these healing gifts.

The gifts of the male experience that we will explore in this final chapter are courage, fortitude, vision, and the capacity for loving service to the world. Each of these gifts from the male soul forms a quest for us as contemporary men, that must be undertaken if we are to forge the potential within ourselves for a new relationship to earth. We will explore the quest for courage through a return to the theme of the hero's journey, as illustrated by Jacob. Courage is the human characteristic that faith in a creating God requires, for over and over again throughout our lives, God summons us with new calls to adventure. Will we be able as Moses was to hear that summons when we are eighty years old, with fresh hope and vigor? Will we have the courage, even then, to undertake new adventures of service? The companion quests that undergird such courage are the hero-warrior's quest for fortitude, the hero-transcendent's quest for vision, and the hero-creative's quest for loving service to world and family. Without undertaking the quest for these gifts, we diminish our lives immeasurably and fail to claim the greatness for which we were created. In fact, without courage, fortitude, vision, and loving service unleashed for the tasks of our time, we will surely perish. As we bring this journey into the male soul to a close, we will look for specific ways to claim each of these gifts.

Discovering the Via Positiva

These quests rest on a new relationship with the earth and with the feminine in our time. I believe that Matthew Fox (1983) has correctly named the necessary originating point for meaningful self-understanding in our time to be a renewed spirit of blessing, hope, pleasure, and appreciation of physical life. He has named this relationship the *via positiva*. In the beginning of Judeo-Christian tradition stands God the creator bringing all things to life and calling all created beings "good." One of the great privileges of my life was to spend a year in a Caribbean setting early in my adult life. Shortly after we were married, my wife, Ruth, and I spent a year on St. John in the U.S. Virgin Islands. There we learned to dance, to laugh, and to live life in a day-to-day presence that we had never known before. We learned the value of deep friendship and discovered the possibility of making time for profound conversation and simple pleasures. We learned to revel in the creation as creatures of the earth. Our renewal as men begins in appreciation of the profound beauty, joy, mystery, and pleasure that are ours as children of the earth. When we begin in such appreciation, we discover that the earth is still Eden. And in our own daily lives, we can touch again the joy of being alive in the flesh. D. H. Lawrence expressed this unfathomable mystery of life in this way:

> For man, the vast marvel is to be alive. For man, as for flower and beast and bird, the supreme triumph is to be most vividly, most perfectly alive. Whatever the unborn and the dead may know they cannot know the beauty, the marvel of being alive in the flesh. The dead may look after the afterwards. But the magnificent here and now

of life in the flesh is ours, and ours alone, and ours only for a time. We ought to dance with rapture that we should be alive and in the flesh, and part of the living, incarnate cosmos. . . . I am part of the great whole, and I can never escape. But I *can* deny my connections, break them, and become a fragment. Then I am wretched.

What we want is to destroy our false inorganic connections, especially those related to money, and re-establish the living organic connections, with the cosmos, the sun and earth, with mankind and nation and family. Start with the sun, and the rest will slowly, slowly happen. (1966, 199–200)

In our age, the time has come to embrace all opposites and to cherish our passions. It is a time to embrace our full natures, physical as well as spiritual, and in this new embrace with the earth to profoundly embrace woman, as well.

Our age calls for every man to look afresh at his relationship with women in the workplace and in the home. The legends of the Holy Grail provide those amazingly unique stories of the variety of relationships with women, in some cases chaste, in some cases passionately embracing. Our age compels us to make peace with the feminine in all her forms, with our mothers, with our mate, with our daughters, and our coworkers. This age of new empowerment for women calls for a profoundly new relationship between men and women, one of wonder, joy, and shared creativity. The beginning place for this new relationship is to make the discovery for ourselves, each and every one, that life is very good. From the wellspring of this goodness, we then bless the woman who bore us in her womb and with whom we first knew the possibility of a union beyond the boundaries of our own unique personality. And we bless the women with whom we have known that union, even fleetingly, in sexual embrace. Above all, we are empowered to envision the creative power of joining with a woman in lifelong commitment to create a home that becomes "a haven of blessing and a place of peace." All of this becomes possible as we fully receive the gift of life in the flesh and claim the partnership of our own creative spirit with the matter of flesh and blood that is ours for this time of life.

There is only one beginning point to life. It is a gift which we must choose to receive. It is nothing less than the gift of all creation in its splendorous magnificence and the gift of love in its surprising joy. It is ours when we see God in every raindrop and flower and bird, when we allow ourselves to be overwhelmed in laughter or in tears by the magnificence of this gift, to be enchanted by its loveliness, and to be filled by its sights and smells and textures, when we awaken to reverence for all moments of life. We cannot, you see, hold any longer the alienation of the hero-transcendent toward the human body and the body's passions, especially its erotic energies, for to do so is to create an unbridgeable chasm between ourselves and earth. We must reclaim our bodies, restore to awareness our emotional needs, and thereby present our whole selves, body and soul, to the tasks of life. When we do so, we are given the creative energy for a lifetime of service to the demanding and eternally creating God.

This new union of body and soul, of flesh and spirit, is perhaps nowhere more vividly represented than in the love between man and woman. We have been created in God's image. And in the joining together of life purpose, goals, values, economic life, and bodies, each couple becomes a center of life and blessing to the world. I have symbolized this new relationship with the embrace of man and woman in Rodin's sculpture *The Kiss* created in the nineteenth century (Figure 13). There is a new creative energy, a new Holy Spirit among us. This spirit calls for a full embrace of the whole being, lest we diminish the value of any creature by diminishing the value within ourselves of any part of our nature. Incarnation blesses every simple passion with joy. We begin our healing by fully embracing earthly life.

There is another embrace that this attitude facilitates. It is the embrace between our own consciousness and the unconscious forces that dwell within us. We live now in an age that in the West has wrestled with a psychological self-understanding of human existence for a century. According to this self-understanding, we are beings in whom there is a surface level of self-awareness, usually called the "ego," and a deeper level, which we often call the "unconscious." The unconscious speaks directly to us through dreams and through intuitive nudges, when we perceive a message that something "feels" right or does not "feel" right. This deeper level of ourselves will find ways to break through into our surface-level self-awareness. How willing we are to listen and to respond to this unconscious self often determines how content we are with our lives. We look in our time to this deeper level of self-awareness to provide the keys to our motivations and the hidden patterns of our actions. This deeper source within is also the residing place of the divine spark within

Fig. 13. Auguste Rodin, The Kiss. Marble, 1886. Paris, Musée Rodin.

ourselves. St. Teresa of Avila in the sixteenth century spoke of God enthroned upon our hearts. She used this image, so that we would "not imagine that we are hollow inside" (Kavanaugh and Rodriguez, 1980, 144).

Our creativity resides in this deeper structure of ourselves. There resides the source of inspiration and of creative discomfort with the limitations of each present moment. The Jungian analyst and writer

Marie-Louise von Franz has eloquently stated the plight of contemporary man with his highly developed ego and weaker awareness of inner depth.

> [The] creatively active aspect of the psychic nucleus can come into play only when the ego gets rid of all purposive and wishful aims and tries to get to a deeper, more basic form of existence. The ego must be able to listen attentively and to give itself, without any further design or purpose, to that inner urge toward growth. Many existentialist philosophers try to describe this state, but they go only as far as stripping off the illusions of consciousness: They go right up to the door of the unconscious and then fail to open it. (1964, 164)

Our age calls for a new marriage within our very selves between the conscious and unconscious forces. This task is not dissimilar to other tasks of reconciliation before us. A psychologist, who has extensive experience with couples, speaks of the relationship between the man and woman as a direct mirror of the relationship for each partner with his or her own unconscious, with his or her own interior life. Thus the key for him to beginning the healing process for a couple is to see the dynamics of the relationship they present in therapy as also indicative of the dynamics internally for each partner with himself or herself. Whatever is alienated within is mirrored in what is alienated without (Culberson 1988). Thus Carl Jung spoke of the deeper source of creativity within us in contrasexual terms, calling this force the feminine "anima" for men and the masculine "animus" for women. The age of a new embrace with all the forces of our lives is upon us. Surrender to God also means a profound surrender into the inner healing of our own psyche. I have given extensive attention to this process in my book *Christian Meditation and Inner Healing* (1991), describing a model for deep inner awareness and many styles of Christian meditation and inner awareness that facilitate contact with this deep creative source within us.

The Quest for Courage: Awakening to the Hero's Journey

Jacob undertook many journeys within his journey: the journey from homeland, the journey into relationship, the journey into his full authority as a man of skill, the journey back home to face Esau, the journey into parenthood, and the journey into God. His model provides a powerful insight for us into the many challenges life presents to us and the courage life requires. Courage is the human quality that faith requires. Forever, we hear a creative and creating God posing new challenges before us. The apostle Paul goes so far as to state that the "inarticulate groans" within our spirit are God speaking through us (Rom. 8). These inarticulate groans of our human spirit are the challenges life places before us as cocreators with God of new life.

Jacob shows us a powerful image of the particular tasks that each man must face. For seven years he indentures himself into the service of Laban in order to win the hand of Rachel in marriage. At the end of this time Laban tricks him into marriage with Leah. That period of Jacob's life is very much like the first decade or so of adult life for us all. We think that we are working toward our heart's desire, but we find that we have actually been living out the internalized expectations of our culture. The work may have been very satisfying and a major contribution to others, yet it has been motivated from a source within ourselves that is not yet fully alive to the deepest level of our unconscious creativity or yet fully alive in God.

During the second period of his adult life, Jacob lives in service of his own heart's desire. This second apprenticeship to life is the one in which he finds his true love manifesting in Rachel. This period may well correspond to that decade or so in our lives in which we begin to find the deeper sources of soul within ourselves, as well as deeper sources of creativity to offer to our work and to our family. The era may be the journey into ourselves facilitated by profound spiritual practice or psychotherapy or a crisis in relationship or vocation that calls us into a new relationship to ourselves.

Finally, Jacob works seven years to build up his wealth. He stays in Laban's service in order to reap the fruit of all his other years of labor. This is the era in which we fully "come of age." It is intriguing that as long as twenty-five hundred years ago in Greece, Solon stated that a man was not really complete until age forty-two. We are finding in our time that this period of genuine empowerment for men is coming certainly no sooner than the forties and often somewhat later. This era is the one beautifully described in Jacob's story as the era of wealth. We may express our wealth not only when our salaries are at their peak but also in the wealth of knowledge, skill, and wisdom we may bring to our world during this era of our lives.

Dante spoke of four stages of adult life. The first he called Adolescence, which occurs until about the age of twenty-five. During Adolescence, we learn the ways of our culture and our family. We learn our trade, we choose an identity. The second stage he called Manhood. During this period, which lasts roughly from the age of twenty-five to forty-five, we raise our families, contribute to our society and simultaneously undertake a deep inner journey of awareness. This dual path, with our lives focused both within the world and within our own inner spirit, prepares us for what Dante called Age, beginning about age forty-five and lasting well into the seventies. In Age we make our most profound contributions to our culture. Then in the seventies or beyond, we enter Decrepitude, able to bless our life with its accomplishments and to turn our attention more and more toward God and the transition into the afterlife (Campbell 1968b, 633–34).

Jacob's life mirrors these stages well, his first years with Laban being his years of early Manhood and his second seven years of service attending to his inner-life development through attention to his heart's love, Rachel. He enters Age, the era of wealth, ready to achieve and contribute to his culture. Yet, all of this is not enough for Jacob, because there is a deep part of himself that was left unfinished in his relationship with Esau. So deep is his need for reconciliation that he has the courage to leave everything aside and once more set out to a new adventure. That is the creative life that courage brings, as we respond again and again to the call to new life that God issues to us.

The Call of the Soul

One of the most courageous journeys any man can be called to undertake is the journey into the deeper parts of himself that we might call the journey into the soul. In contemporary Western culture, so much of our attention is directed outward into the realm of achievement in the world that we have become quite alienated from our own inner depths. I observe this phenomenon more in men than in women. Except in unusual circumstances in which there is a direct vocational expression for the inner life, such as in psychotherapy, counseling, and ministry, men seem to be participants in activities related to inner-life development much less frequently than women. In a typical retreat for meditation or self-exploration, one will often find a much higher percentage of women than men.

What this means for us as men is that it is often only in the most dramatic forms, such as a major midlife crisis, that we begin to attend to the deeper and unexpressed parts of ourselves. For this reason, I suggest, the inner journey into ourselves is a hero's journey requiring courage to undertake.

We often do not even recognize that our deep boredoms and fears, rages and quiet desperations might be messages from our deeper selves and from God, inviting us into a process of self-examination and change. Carl Jung's distinction between the conscious and the unconscious parts of ourselves is a very useful place to begin our understanding of this call of the soul. For Jung, the "unconscious" is simply that which is unknown regarding the inner world (Jung 1968a, §2). The "ego" or the "I" is that which is known. The unknown of the inner world, or the unconscious, falls into two major categories, the personal unconscious and what he called the transpersonal or collective unconscious (Jung 1966, §103).

The self in Jung's writings is finally unknown, dissolving the boundary between individual consciousness and God, yet it is knowable in part (Jung 1968a, §9). The first task of listening for the call of the soul is to become aware that there is a greater self within ourselves than we consciously know. Do we identify ourselves, our "I," merely with our habitual ways of being, or do we dare to address ourselves to the unknown within? The self for Jung is the bridge between the personal "I" and the infinite potentiality represented by the collective or transpersonal realms. This self in Jung is very close to the soul of Western spiritual life. Jung calls upon us to discover a "mid-point of the personality" that is capable of consciously assimilating material that has been previously unconscious to us. "This would be the point of new equilibrium, a new centering of the total personality, a virtual centre which, on account of its focal position between conscious and unconscious, ensures for the personality a new and more solid foundation" (Jung 1966, §365). The courage to become more than we have been, even within our own self-awareness, inspires us toward the hero's journey of inner-life awakening.

In the earliest Western use of the word *psyche* in the *Iliad*, the term simply meant what leaves a man in death. It would in this usage be very similar to the meaning of *zoë*. "When a spear strikes the heart of a warrior, and his *psyche* dissolves (5:296), is destroyed (22:325), or simply leaves him (16:453), or is coughed out through the mouth (9:409), or bled out through a wound (14:518; 16:505), there is nothing whatever about time or about the end of anything" (Jaynes 1976, 271). Later, *psyche* comes to be identified "with that which exists after life has ceased" (289), the shades of afterlife. In this form, the soul is familiar to Western thought in its view of a continuity of life between this world and the afterlife.

What I am suggesting is that one of our great life tasks is to open our own self-awareness to the depths within ourselves, and in so doing begin to rediscover a new depth of soul. We can begin by understanding the soul not simply as an otherworldly appendage to this life. Instead, the concept of soul describes the experience of coming into relationship with our whole selves, making a bridge between our own inner realms of darkness and light. For men, it may be most useful to remember that in Greek thought *psyche* or soul was identified as a beautiful young woman, the paramour of Eros. We may think of the soul as the feminine nature within ourselves. Such an identification enables us to enter into relationship with this other dimension of ourselves and to have the full range of relationship with our soul that we might enjoy with another person. The soul, indeed, is lover, guide, companion, taskmaster, and playmate. Once awakened, she requires companionship and is a jealous lover.

Further clarifications are supplied in Figure 14. If we take the active masculine principle to be the primary thrust of the ego in encountering the world in action, then undergirding this active dimension is a realm of interior experience that leads both back toward birth and forward toward death. The kinds of experience contained in the soul may range from memories of birth and early childhood to visions of death and divine inspiration. Within the soul lies the capacity for healing of memories, discovery of the emotional roots of diseases, and the intervention of divine epiphanies. This expanded realm of human consciousness, this soul, is the arena illuminated by mythic and sacred story, where the individual egoic-self is in direct contact with the heroic tasks of collective human life. As the stories of mythology or scripture awaken a deeper self-awareness, we may contact realms of light and darkness and do battle with our own time's questions of health and disease, good and evil.

What this model of consciousness suggests is that the soul can call to the egoic mind of the male, thrusting toward achievement in the world, through a number of channels. She can come to us in

WORLD OF ACTION

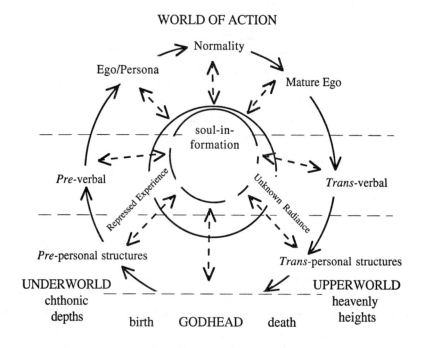

Fig. 14. Adapted by permission of the publisher from Ken Wilber, *The Atman Project* (Wheaton, Ill.: Theosophical Publishing House, Quest Books, 1980), p. 50.

physiological distress patterns. She can come in dreams and night visions of terror dredging up repressed material, or she can come in visions and dreams of radiance and divine guidance. When she calls, will we answer her and begin to enter into relationship with her, or will we ignore her and continue our aggressive achievement-oriented lifestyles unchanged? A theory arises from our study: when we consistently ignore the voices of the soul coming to us in dreams, longings, and visions of light, we may directly contribute to bringing stress-related diseases upon ourselves. Our interiority will beckon us. Our rejection will put further enmity between our waking con-

sciousness and our depths. Or we may begin a relationship of courtship and mutual partnership. We must learn to treat our own inner
urgings with the same respect that the divine was treated in mythic
and sacred story.

> What finds expression in [mythic story] is the faith that the known
> and disposable world in which man lives does not have its ground and
> aim in itself, but in the uncanny powers that lie outside of what is
> known and disposable and constantly control and threaten it as its
> ground and limit. In unity with this, myth also expresses the knowl-
> edge that man is not lord over himself, and that he is not only depen-
> dent within the known world, but is especially dependent upon the
> powers that hold sway beyond it. (Bultmann 1961, 10–11)

So, too, for each man, we undertake the tasks of surrender to that
which is greater and beyond the conscious self-production of our
lives.

The call of the soul may not at first be pleasant. She may come
in the form of the Loathly Damsel. In such a form she came to me.
This crisis of self-identity came at the age of thirty-four and was
accompanied by a remarkable dream. In the dream, I was at a
picnic, sitting on the ground with a colleague, when suddenly the
grass turned to snakes. I awoke terrified. I now perceive that dream
as the call of the soul to me. It was the call of the unconscious and
repressed parts of myself shaking me into a new self-awareness. The
soul used the image of the primordial snake and my own terror of
the snake to shake me into a deeper awareness of myself.

I feel blessed to have answered the call of the soul, even in this
terrifying form. Over the next few years, the snake became no longer
a source of terror, but rather a guide and barometer for the soul-
work in which I was engaged. In one dream the snake approached
my wife, threatening to kill her, and I killed the snake. That event
seemed very important. It was a statement of my waking rational
consciousness that there were boundaries to this flooding of my
consciousness with unconscious material. I would allow only so
much in. I would not allow it to threaten my primary relationship.
At the time there was also a good deal of upheaval within myself in
regard to my relational life, and so the dream powerfully reinforced
my own conscious intention to ride through this awakening of the
soul with my wife as partner. I would also say that my wife represented the higher feminine within me, and the snake represented

the chthonic Great Mother. I was willing to enter into relationship with the chthonic, but not at the expense of the loss of the higher, spiritual self.

In another dream, I was surrendering to be struck in the forehead by a snake. By moving into relationship with the forehead and "third-eye," the snake in this dream was beckoning me to a new quality of spiritual life. Such an awakening is often accompanied by difficult psychological distress or purification (Underhill 1961). Within the dream I was surrendering. Outside of the dream, however, my rational mind was suffering. I was making so much noise in my sleep that I awoke my wife, and she nudged me awake just before the snake struck. Perhaps in that action we affirmed that we would awake to these spiritual energies together without losing our relationship or our self-identities.

In another dream I was visited by a snake, and I swept it out the door, thereby establishing a mutual respect. Yet another dream was like an initiation. It was set in a primitive tribal atmosphere. A man brought a snake up from the ground and held it at my mouth. Without fear, I endured its closeness. Then I took the snake and returned it to the ground. That dream occurred about the time I began psychotherapy. I was passing the initiation rite of psychotherapy, bringing to expression my repressed depths: my fears and tears and rages. In another, I went to a pet store to shop for a snake and bought a case for it, which was like an incense burner. The dream indicated that I had begun to establish a clear relationship with the snake and the realms of the unconscious to which I was being awakened.

Another dream took me to a hellish realm, with one snake very large and fat on the ground, and another coiled around the head of a priestlike male figure. The large snake on the ground seemed much like a penis. The energies were now differentiating. I could encounter the serpent in its sexual, earthy form, and in its heavenly, enlightening form. In another dream, I discovered an old black man wearing a hat with a bronze snake on it going to church. Here, the dark chthonic and the possible energy of enlightenment joined in a wonderful reconciliation. I was astonished to find the man's hat somewhat later on the cover of Michael Harner's *The Way of the Shaman* (1982). I also made peace with my childhood memory of snakes. There was an area at my grandparents' barnyard that attracted snakes. In a dream, I walked at leisure among many coiled, lethargic snakes. Another dream showed the caduceus, a vision of hope for wholeness, toward which the soul was drawing me.

In my case, the soul called clearly from the chthonic realm. My awakening was prompted by the Great Mother or the Loathly Damsel. It was the primal, instinctual energy to which my attention was drawn. A primary path for me in coming to know my soul has been the body. Learning to live with the energies of the body, particularly its lower passions: sexual and aggressive. In terms of the mythic images we have been studying, my egoic self was well versed in the ways of the hero-transcendent. What wholeness required of me was to come into contact with the warrior energies. My midlife call of the soul came from the repressed material from childhood and the awakened energies of the body. In liberating these lower energies, however, the higher energies have also awakened: the energies of the spiritual radiance as well as direct communion with the inner Christ.

The awakening of the soul may come for other men primarily from the heavenly realms. Such has been the case for a forty-eight-year-old businessman with whom I am acquainted. For twenty-five years, he has devoted himself to building a business, starting without capital. It has required tremendous effort, and many times he has been close to bankruptcy. He has spent many of these years in tortured anxiety, lest the business should fail. In the last few years, however, his night visions have taken on the form of an encounter with God. He awakens in a state of awareness of divine presence, sometimes engaging in what feels like a wrestling match with God. These episodes often involve heightened breathing and the extension of his arms in tension. Throughout these experiences there has consistently been a conclusion that gives him a sense of peace and assurance that his business venture is divinely inspired and that he can trust it to continue despite the difficulties. A few years ago, he was drawn to begin a regular meditation practice and to undertake an intensive study of the spiritual writings of Western mystics. His call from the soul came not from the chthonic, but from the Queen of Heaven. In his case, as well as mine, there has been a reorientation to the body, a release from chronic tensions, and a new ease of presence to inner visioning of spiritual figures. This process of reorientation to the body's energies in times of spiritual awakening has been given considerable attention by many schools of bodywork in recent years. *Job's Body* (Juhan 1987) is one of the most comprehensive discussions of bodywork. Much of the theoretical basis for these new therapies has been described by Alexander Lowen in his many books.

When the soul calls, we may find ourselves in need of a guide to assist in the process. In my case, I sought a great deal of guidance, in psychotherapy, in various meditation teachings, and in forms of bodywork. In the case of the man called from the heavenly realms, he largely found his way on his own. His own self-directed reading in mystic writings has given him many insights to assist him in making sense of his experience. We are wise to recall that this awakening is difficult, and that it leads inevitably to some form of dismemberment of our previous self-identity. We can greatly assist the process by sharing our awakening with others who have had similar experiences and by seeking the guidance of those who have traversed this path within themselves. Recent attention to the phenomena associated with spiritual emergence and spiritual emergency has been most useful (Bragdon 1990; Grof 1989 and 1990).

The Sirens, in Greek mythology, present one of the most powerful images of the dangers of this awakening. The Sirens, surely one of the sweetest voices of the soul, call men to shipwreck. Let us join the Argonauts after the completion of an adventure:

> The Argo sped on in a fresh breeze, and soon they saw a beautiful island, green and flower-laden, the habitation of the beguiling sirens, who lure passers-by with their singing, but only to destroy them. Half bird and half maiden, they always lay in wait for new quarry, and no one who came near could escape them. Now they sang their sweetest airs to the Argonauts, who were just about to cast their rope ashore and make fast the ship, when Orpheus, the singer from Thrace, rose in his seat and began to strike such rich and ringing chords on the strings of his divine lyre that he drowned out the voices decoying his friends to death. (Schwab 1946, 130–31)

As we undertake to answer the call of the soul, we will want to recall that ensouling is a process of destructuring, involving major changes in self-awareness and identity. But it is not only a destructuring, it is also the task of listening for a new song from Orpheus, from the divine center within ourselves. Here, the Grail quest is helpful to remember. Our Western heritage does not particularly encourage us to undertake the interior quest simply for its own sake, but rather to undertake it as a part of the quest for our unique mode of service to humanity. At some point, that quest may require a deep interior journey and dismemberment. But the purpose of that dismemberment is to hear God's song afresh in our hearts. It is not simply to death that we are called but to new forms of health.

> Midway this way of life we're bound upon,
> I woke to find myself in a dark wood,
> Where the right road was wholly lost and gone.
> (Dante 1949, 71, *L'Inferno* I:1–3)

As Dante found his life disrupted by this call of the soul, so may each of us. If she calls, we will hopefully answer. We may find ourselves involved in major relocations, job searches, periods of retreat, or domestic upheaval. However, if we heed this call, we may find ourselves well prepared to offer truly beneficent gifts of creative service to the world, springing out of the creative essence of God. "'After our own proper perfection, which is acquired in manhood,' Dante writes, 'that perfection should also come which enlightens not only ourselves, but others'" (Campbell 1968b, 634).

Thus the midlife crisis is nothing new. No doubt, it was familiar to Abraham, Jacob, and Moses, when they heard the call to new forms of life. Jesus must have occasioned it in all the disciples, whose lives he disrupted. It has been with humankind for at least three thousand years. I suggest, however, it is not properly named. Its name more clearly stated is *the call of the soul.*

This model points to the theme we have been exploring in the Grail quest: that Western life is focused on the individual coming into creative partnership with God and, from one's individual life, offering unique contributions for the renewal of society. In the West, social structures have been unstable. The centuries-old traditions of "caste" have been broken. Now each individual is expected to enter creatively into the renewal of his society throughout each stage of his life. The Western model teaches us that, "you have a great responsibility. . . . You are a throw of the dice on which, for a moment, the entire fate of your race is gambled" (Kazantzakis 1960b, 72). The model for midlife is Moses, going forth on his quest to the mountain top, not only for himself but for the good of the whole community. It is vitally important to the well-being of Western society that a man undergo a significant awakening of soul in midlife, so that he can offer his contributions of wisdom to his culture in his later years.

Awakening to Wholeness

As the model of consciousness in Figure 14 suggests, there is a range of interior awareness available to each human being that is usually known only in a minimal way. Our midlife awakening will be an explosion of consciousness into realms of the interior from which we have heretofore been cut off. For some this will be an influx of energies from the underworld or the prepersonal world, that world that contains the primal energies of our instinctual physical life. This world has been the province of classical psychoanalysis, opening us up to the repressed parts of ourselves as well as the repressed memories of childhood. Much energy for life is to be gained here. From an evolutionary standpoint, this is the realm of the hero-warrior. The hero-warrior of history lived very alive to these primal energies and the passions of physical awareness, sexuality, and aggression. As we open to our interior, we may well find an awakening to these fierce energies.

Another form of awakening is associated with the upperworld or the transpersonal world. This is preeminently the world of the historic hero-transcendent. It is a world that is awakened in our time through meditative spiritual practice. It is a realm where we may come to know transcendent entities such as the inner Christ or the Blessed Virgin as trustworthy inner guides when we seek discernment. It is the realm that the mystics of the ages have identified with a direct perception of God in experiences of radiant light or benevolent dark. It is a realm often beyond words for it takes us into the direct perception of the experience of "life as such."

A third kind of awakening in midlife may be a new vigor of the rational and creative minds. This new vigor of creative imagination is the realm of the hero-creative interfacing the inner world with the needs of the external world. We may find fresh joy in contributing in loving service to our families, neighborhoods, and political structures. This awakening creativity may manifest in writing projects or projects of creative expression with arts or hobbies. It is the world of action impacted by a new inner depth. This is the world of the ego, of normality, interacting with the world, described in Figure 14. It shows what possibilities await us when the "soul-in-formation" deepens within ourselves, yet also manifests in an outward thrust into the world.

All three awakenings are likely to come in midlife. Wherever we

begin this journey, its natural movement is to take us toward the
new center of personality, hovering between the conscious and unconscious worlds. From this new center, we claim the wholeness
that we are and bring that totality into creative engagement with
the needs of the world.

The Quest for Fortitude:
Awakening the Hero-Warrior

What I have come to know
is the burning, searing,
smoldering
Holy Rage
that is my molten
core.

Beneath all veneers
in the center of my being
lies the sun
in inexhaustible energy
enlightening, judging,
flashing—

I see that my exhaustion
in the past in holy deeds
resides more in my closing down
on this incredibly
strong power
within myself,
rather than—as I had
supposed—
in serving it too much.
I have created of myself
a pressured
volcanic time-bomb.

The question is not
whether there shall
be a molten core

of light and heat
and explosive power
within me.

The question is whether
I shall be a smoldering
volcano—never fully exploding
in passion
or whether I shall come
into the fullness of my
power—
and spew forth heat
and light
and flaming passion
to those who live
with me in this
fragile moment
in human history—

Love
is passionate presence.

Those words came to me at a time of profound awakening to the powerful energies of the underworld, a direct perception of the fierceness that resides in the energy of my own aggression. During a powerful group breathwork experience, along with the physical awareness of this aggressive energy, came the vision of the ancient warrior, the sword-wielding warrior of righteousness. I also saw the symbol of the caduceus, with its intertwined healing serpents. The vision culminated with a healing perspective on the world. So, while receiving my own most direct experience of the powerful underworld energies of aggression, I simultaneously grasped that this power was to be used in healing for the world.

What my experience suggests is that the soul calls us to wholeness and desires to give both transcendent vision along with the awakening of our full masculine power. In our Western culture the warrior as warrior of righteousness has been much neglected in recent years. We witnessed the power of this warrior of righteousness in the civil rights revolution of the sixties. Yet, in the nineties, we allow our cities to decay and our homeless problems to go unchecked. We seem to have lost our national resolve to perfect our society. The holy warrior of history will not stand by timidly while such decay goes on.

The warrior tradition found its completion in the prophetic tradition of the Old Testament, where lone individuals were willing to stand completely apart from the prevailing culture and say: Thus saith the Lord, repent, change your ways! The warrior finds completion in this extraordinary vision of Jesus in the book of Revelation:

> I turned to see whose voice it was that spoke to me; and when I turned I saw seven standing lamps of gold, and among the lamps one like a son of man, robed down to his feet, with a golden girdle round his breast. The hair of his head was white as snow-white wool, and his eyes flamed like fire; his feet gleamed like burnished brass refined in a furnace, and his voice was like the sound of rushing waters. In his right hand he held seven stars, and out of his mouth came a sharp two-edged sword; and his face shone like the sun in full strength. (Rev. 1:12–16, NEB)

Can we claim this powerful source of energy within us?

I believe this deep power is what Robert Bly is suggesting that men need to claim. Without it, we have lost one of the most dynamic legacies of the Western male experience, the power to change reality by tapping into the dynamic energy source within ourselves. It requires tremendous resolve to be the warrior of righteousness, to tackle the structural problems of our time and to stay with the process until change happens.

The word that speaks to this awakened power as well as to the capacity to endure years of effort at a task is an old word, a word seldom heard these days, the word *fortitude*. It comes from the Latin word for strong. It is courage that can endure. We desperately need fortitude to face the problems of our age. I suggest that fortitude is the capacity that we find well honed in the historic hero-warrior. Not only is there within this warrior the awakening of powerful aggressive energies that can break out in violence. There is also the enlightened aggression that can change the course of history. What the awakened warrior needs to guide him is the vision of the hero-transcendent. But without the power of the warrior's energy and fortitude, the vision of the hero-transcendent can remain only an inward vision and not find its way to outward expression.

We may think of this quest for the fortitude of the hero-warrior as taking the mask off of our aggressive energies within the context of a prayer of surrender to God, so that this power be used for the health of our society and our world. Without this context, then we have only liberated a personal energy that can follow far too easily in the footsteps of Hercules and turn at any moment against the innocents around us. Perhaps the new men's movement will ultimately tackle the problems of urban blight, the squandering of our youths' lives in drugs, and the violence of the gangs that are making combat zones of our cities.

We might theorize that men highly troubled with violence are warriors without a cause, or with a cause so focused in momentary self-gratification that it resembles Hercules' periodic outbursts against his loved ones. We may begin to heal the random violence of our culture by claiming the power of this aggression afresh and turning it toward the amelioration of social problems. The problem is not that within us lies this molten core of violent power; the problem is that there is no clear place for this warrior energy to be utilized in our time. We must remember that for three thousand years one of the honored classes of men has been the warrior class. Within this century, this warrior has found dishonor. The archetypal energy of the warrior now desperately needs a clear mission, a mission of healing. The energy of the hero-warrior can be used for great good if it is acknowledged and channeled toward healing for the world. We must release the warrior of righteousness with fresh energy into civic life.

The Quest for Vision: Awakening the Hero-Transcendent

Our time brings forward into popular life the opportunity for us each to awaken the realms of profound intuition and insight that the mystics have reported through the ages. In this era of "the serpent coiled around the sun," I have suggested that access to the transpersonal realities may be available with much less arduous rigor than attended the early monastics of the Christian era. If this is the era in which God is directly communing with individual human beings, as foretold in the vision of the book of Revelation, then we might expect a more direct knowing of divine guidance than in past eras of human history. Although I cannot prove that this is the age thus foretold, it seems to me that there are signs of such a deepening personal awareness and connection with divine inspiration.

For the first time in human history, the pathways of inner knowledge are available in any good religious bookstore. The meditative pathways are well described, their practices elucidated for all to read (cf. Goldstein 1987; Goleman 1988; Judy 1991; Kelsey 1976; Pennington 1980; Ram Dass 1978; Radha 1978). Teachers of many spiritual traditions abound. Within Christian tradition, resources long hidden in the monasteries are now available, as many religious orders have opened their doors for silent and guided retreats. The process of spiritual emergence is again being described with precision for individuals of our time.

What all of this attention to inner-life development suggests is that there is a deep hunger for finding a new depth of relationship to the divine. We are as a people engaged in a massive quest for vision to sustain us in our time of historic change. This era is particularly demanding upon humankind. We have entered the era of the global village. We instantaneously know the triumphs and the sufferings of people around the world. Were we to take upon ourselves the challenge to respond meaningfully to every suffering of which we hear, we could not do so. Compassion seeks a new definition when my neighbor is as surely around the world as next door. The global village demands fresh vision for each of us in terms of how we will utilize our energy for the good of the earth. A new challenge in discernment is presenting itself to us.

The history of the hero-transcendent offers some guidance to us. One of the mainstays of the hero-transcendent of history has been the capacity to stand over and apart from one's culture. The way in which this separation has been cultivated is through retreat. Sometimes in the dramatic form of a physical separation into the hermitage or into the monastery, sometimes in less dramatic forms, such as the annual retreat for discernment required in the Roman Catholic priesthood, there is an understanding within the life of the hero-transcendent that time out from the world must happen in order to attune to the deeper movement of the Holy Spirit. I want to suggest that this process of retreat, whether structured or unstructured, is essential for each of us in our time.

I find for myself that the few weeks around Christmas have taken on this quality over the last few years. In the darkest time of the year, there is for me a natural inward turning. I find myself making more time in my daily activities for introspective writing in my journal. I find myself thinking about the year ahead of me and making priorities of the tasks that might take on my energy. I think that some cycle of discernment like this is truly essential in our time. We may find resources for this task in meditation, in journal writing, in dream work, and in direct work clarifying our values and our priorities. In recent years, personal goal setting has come of age as a discipline for discerning life direction through attention to our core values. Some of these processes of values clarification and goal setting are very useful to undertake (Covey 1989; Fadiman 1989).

We may also find special opportunities for retreat in nature or in guided experiences of meditation and personal renewal. All of these allow the space to listen for a deeper discernment of our vision as it changes from season to season in our lives. The model of the hero's journey suggests that the call to adventure will come in new forms from time to time, setting our life energy in fresh directions. Our task is to make time within our life to listen for this movement of divine inspiration.

One of the other profound methods for discernment that Western spiritual life created was attention to the seven deadly sins. These are interior motivations and attitudes that tend to set our actions into certain directions. Growing out of the original temptations of Jesus in the wilderness, they were further clarified into the seven deadly attitudes of pride, envy, wrath, sloth, covetousness, gluttony, and lust. By the time Dante incorporated these into the *Divine Comedy*, in his *Purgatory*, they had become differentiated into active forms of hatred toward one's neighbor, or misplaced love of good (1955, 62). Through this framework, the medieval mind thought very carefully regarding interior attitudes and subtle motivations. Regrettably, in our time we have often neglected this attention to the connection between interior motivation and exterior action. If we lust after a bigger house, we are more than likely to think only of our economic options, rather than to consider carefully the moral implications of such a move. The hero-transcendent invites us to genuine and healthy introspection of our motives, asking us where our actions are leading us not only for the present but for the future as well. We see this attention to interior motivation recurring in the ecological crisis in our time. But accustomed as we have become in the West to weighing our decisions in light primarily of economics, we have much interior knowledge to gain by looking more deeply at the attitudes that draw us from within.

Without vision and discernment, the hero-warrior's aggressive energy is usually highly destructive. The combination of the hero-warrior's awakened power with the discerning vision of the hero-transcendent gives us the possibility of a wholehearted relationship to ourselves, to our world, and to God. This is the whole man that the "voice out of the whirlwind" demanded that Job become, before the direct relationship with God would be given. "Stand up like a man, and then I will speak to you," the divine voice said. Stand up, take on your full capacity as a man, the capacity for power, the capacity for vision, and then God will address you face to face.

The Quest for Loving Service: Awakening the Hero-Creative

The awakened man, however, is not complete in and of himself. Western tradition, mythic and spiritual, points to the need for completing the solitary life in relationship with society and culture. Perhaps Dante's stages of life, in which attention is given to the capacity for profound service in the period of Age, is truly the hidden model for Western life. Christianity requires loving service as the outcome of inner awareness. There is no place for spiritual ecstasy apart from concern for the moral good of the society. We find, whether we look to Christianity or to the Grail quest or to our Hebrew roots, that everywhere humankind is invited to bring vision into society. The prize of the hero's journey is not complete until it has become a boon for the good of others as well.

This capacity for service in our time needs a new relationship to the feminine to find its fullest potential. This new relationship to the feminine runs throughout the male quest. It is a passionately erotic call to love the earth and all things earthly. If we do not reestablish our relationship, our physical relationship, with the earth, we will abuse her until we have substantially altered her. We begin this reconnection by the erotic joining of our own bodies into the love of all other creatures. By erotic, I mean appreciation for our sexual feelings, but I mean much more. Outside my window today is pouring a drought-quenching rain, rain such as I have not seen in six to seven years, sustaining rain. To revel in that rain, as well as in mountain snow, and in ocean shore, to immerse ourselves in the bounty and the mystery of nature is the erotic relationship to the earth that is demanded in our time. It is the relationship that springs forth from appreciation of our bodies and of our body, the earth, as the dwelling place of divine mystery.

The new relationship with the feminine also requires men to become cocreators with women in the workplace. There is an unnamed and often underutilized synergy of men and women as creative coworkers. As men and women become copartners in the workplace, we ought to celebrate the new possibilities for creative expression of health to our world that comes from the joining of complementary skills. This new relationship between men and women promises a revolution toward health which we have never experienced before.

And there is the potential for intimacy in the relationship between man and woman. Can we not claim afresh the medieval wedding vow, "With this ring I thee wed, with my body I thee worship?" In so bringing the climate of joy and full-bodied awareness into our relationship of commitment and love, we forge the possibility of enabling our homes to become new centers of creativity and blessing to our world.

The hero-creative begins with such devoted love to the world and to society, and from the marriage of his whole being to the time in which he lives, he receives the courage and the passionate energy needed to sustain acts of significant service. Our time calls for the fortitude of the hero-warrior, the vision of the hero-transcendent, and the loving service of the hero-creative.

Where will you place the "talent" you have been given? We must ask that question afresh each day, each year. Where will you focus the potential for creative action that is yours? Those are the questions before the man and woman of our time. I think we do not improve on the answer given by Isaiah twenty-five hundred years ago, "Here am I, Lord, send me."

Send me into the village square, send me into the schools, send me into the day camps for children, send me into the task of creating beauty, send me into the business world to create more jobs, send me into the political world to struggle for the values I hold dear, send me into the earth as her son, to love her and to cherish her. Send me to help create the "thousand healths and hidden isles" not even yet imagined. Then I will know that I have lived and loved well with this precious gift of life that has been given to me.

Experiential Questions

1. Return to your notes on the hero's journey in the exercises in chapter 1. Review the responses you gave and now restate the call to adventure, the tests and helpers, the prize, the threshold struggles, and the elixir, adding new understandings from the other exercises of the book.

2. Write a story of your current journey. Use the notes from chapter 1 and from their amplification in the exercise above. You might begin, "Once upon a time." You can write it like a fairy tale using imaginal creatures or like a story using living or imaginary people. Begin with a few sentences. Perhaps it will grow to a page or more. Give it a title.

3. Look over your notes from the exercises of all the chapters. Notice which ones have an emotional charge for you, either positive or negative. These may give you some insight into issues that remain to be completed in the six tasks of mature masculinity: 1) leaving home and making peace with mother; 2) making peace with father in the contest of the hero-warrior with the world; 3) going to the wilderness; 4) making peace with woman in a wide range of relationships; 5) making peace with man in a wide range of relationships; 6) making peace with God.

4. Serve as "spiritual director" to yourself, recommending ways to complete the tasks listed above in number 3. You might consider a form of psychotherapy or counseling or bodywork. You might undertake a spiritual practice or a physical discipline. You might consider using a time-management practice of making more time for leisure and play activities or cultivating relationships for support and colleagueship. Some tasks might involve new forms of community service. If you have the opportunity, discuss these plans with a trusted friend or small group.

5. What is your vision for the world? What is your part in bringing about that vision? What do you want to leave as your legacy to the future?

EPILOGUE

Law of the New Age

I, the Lord your God, am the One who brings you out of every bondage into liberty. You shall have no other gods before me.

The earth is your Mother, who gives you life and nourishes you. You shall worship Her alongside me in holy reverence.

All people, indeed all creatures, are the same in our sight. There are no distinctions.

Therefore, you shall not trespass against any person or creature, especially not against the Earth Herself by threatening Her with nuclear destruction or ecological decay. You shall not support warfare nor the building up of arms.

In order that these laws may be written upon your hearts, and you shall gain further wisdom within, you shall faithfully practice the spiritual disciplines of prayer and meditation. All that you need has already been given in the many spiritual traditions. Choose a path and faithfully follow it.

You shall enjoy the commerce of human society, receiving just wages for your work, and freely spending and giving that which you earn, so that others may also enjoy the gifts of commerce.

You shall join with your mate, your lover, in ecstatic union, celebrating in your union, my own union with Earth Mother. Open yourself to the ecstasy of union, physically and spiritually, that joy may flow out of your life as a blessing to your children, your children's children, and your neighbors.

These laws I give to you for the New Age that your lives may be full of peace and joy, and that you may live long and fruitfully upon the Earth.

> Death Valley
> Vision Quest
> March 1982

REFERENCES

Achterberg, J. 1990. *Woman as healer.* Boston: Shambhala.

à Kempis, T. 1955. *The imitation of Christ.* Edited by H. C. Gardiner, S.J. Garden City, N.Y.: Doubleday.

A Monk of New Clairvaux. 1979. *Don't you belong to me?* New York: Paulist.

Augustine, St. 1950. *The city of God.* Translated by M. Dods. New York: Random House.

———. 1961. *Confessions.* Translated by R. S. Pine-Coffin. Middlesex, Eng.: Penguin.

Blair, E. 1975. *Abingdon Bible handbook.* Nashville and New York: Abingdon.

Bly, R. 1990. *Iron John: A book about men.* Reading, Mass.: Addison-Wesley.

Bragdon, E. 1990. *The call of spiritual emergency.* San Francisco: Harper & Row.

Bultmann, R. 1961. *Kerygma and myth.* Translated by R. H. Fuller. Edited by H. W. Bartsch. New York: Harper Torchbooks.

Campbell, J. 1962. *The masks of God, II: Oriental mythology.* New York: Viking.

———. 1964. *The masks of God, III: Occidental mythology.* New York: Viking.

———. 1968a. *The hero with a thousand faces,* 2nd ed. Princeton, N.J.: Princeton University Press.

———. 1968b. *The masks of God, IV: Creative mythology.* New York: Viking.

———. 1969. *The masks of God, I: Primitive mythology.* New York: Viking.

———. 1981. *The mythic image.* Princeton, N.J.: Princeton University Press.

Capra, F. 1975. *The tao of physics: An exploration of the parallels between modern physics and Eastern mysticism.* New York: Bantam.

Carniero, R. 1980. Chimera of the upper Amazon. In *The don Juan papers: Further Castaneda controversies.* Edited by R. de Mille, 94–98. Santa Barbara, Calif.: Ross-Erickson.

Covey, S. 1989. *The seven habits of highly effective people: Restoring the character ethic.* New York: Simon & Schuster.

Culberson, C. (1988). Personal communication to author.

Dante Alighieri. 1949. *The comedy of Dante Alighieri, the Florentine, cantica I, Hell (L'Inferno).* Translated by D. L. Sayers. New York: Penguin.

———. 1955. *The comedy of Dante Alighieri, the Florentine, cantica II, Purgatory (Il Purgatorio).* Translated by D. L. Sayers. New York: Penguin.

———. 1962. *The comedy of Dante Alighieri, the Florentine, cantica III, Paradise (Il Paradiso).* Translated by D. L. Sayers and B. Reynolds. New York: Penguin.

de la Croix, H. and R. C. Tansey. 1970. *Gardner's art through the ages,* 5th ed. New York: Harcourt, Brace, and World.

de Mille, R., ed. 1980. *The don Juan papers: Further Castaneda controversies.* Santa Barbara, Calif.: Ross-Erickson.

Eisler, R. 1987. *The chalice and the blade: Our history, our future.* San Francisco: Harper & Row.

Eliade, M. 1964. *Shamanism: Archaic techniques of ecstasy.* Translated by W. R. Trask. Princeton, N.J.: Princeton University Press.

———. 1967. *From primitives to zen: A thematic sourcebook of the history of religions.* New York: Harper & Row.

———. 1978. *A history of religious ideas: From stone age to the Eleusinian mysteries,* vol. 1. Translated by W. R. Trask. Chicago: University of Chicage Press.

———. 1982. *A history of religious ideas: From Gautama Buddha to the triumph of Christianity,* vol. 2. Translated by W. R. Trask. Chicago: University of Chicago Press.

Fadiman, J. 1989. B *Unlimit your life: Setting & getting goals.* Berkeley, Calif.: Celestial Arts.

Fields, R. 1991. *The code of the warrior in history, myth, and everyday life.* New York: HarperCollins.

Fox, M. 1980. *Breakthrough: Meister Eckhart's creation spirituality in new translation.* Garden City, N.Y.: Doubleday.

———. 1983. *Original blessing: A primer in creation spirituality.* Santa Fe, N.M.: Bear & Co.

Fuller, R. B. 1981. *Critical path.* New York: St. Martin's.

Furnish, P. V. 1972. *The love command in the New Testament.* Nashville and New York: Abingdon.

Goldscheider, L. 1941. *Donatello.* New York: Oxford University Press, Phaidon edition.

Goldstein, J. 1987. *The experience of insight: A simple and direct guide to Buddhist meditation.* Boston: Shambhala.

Goleman, D. 1988. *The meditative mind: The varieties of the meditative experience.* Los Angeles: J. P. Tarcher.

Grimm Brothers. 1972. *The complete Grimm's fairy tales.* New York: Pantheon.

Grof, C. and S. 1990. *The stormy search for the self: A guide to personal growth through transformational crisis.* Los Angeles: J. P. Tarcher.

Grof, S. 1975. *Realms of the human unconscious: Observations from LSD research.* New York: Viking.

Grof, S. and C., eds. 1989. *Spiritual emergency: When personal transformation becomes a crisis.* Los Angeles: J. P. Tarcher.

Hamilton, E. 1969. *Mythology.* New York: New American Library.

Hand, R. 1981. *Horoscope symbols.* Rockport, Mass.: Para Research.

Harner, M. 1982. *The way of the shaman: A guide to power and healing.* New York: Bantam.

Hibbard, H. 1966. *Masterpieces of Western sculpture from medieval to modern.* New York: Harper & Row.

Hillman, J. 1975. *Re-visioning psychology.* New York: Harper & Row.

Janson, H. W., with D. J. Janson. 1969. *History of art: A survey of the major visual arts from the dawn of history to the present day,* rev. ed. New York: Harry N. Abrams.

Jaynes, J. 1976. *The origin of consciousness in the breakdown of the bicameral mind.* Boston: Houghton Mifflin.

Johnson, R. 1974. *He!* King of Prussia, Penn.: Religious Publishing.

Johnston, W., ed. 1973. *The cloud of unknowing and the book of privy counseling.* Garden City, N.Y.: Doubleday.

Judy, D. 1991. *Christian meditation and inner healing.* New York: Crossroad.

Juhan, D. 1987. *Job's body: A handbook for bodywork*, edited by G. Quasha. Barrytown, N.Y.: Station Hill Press.

Jung, C. G. 1966. *Two essays on analytical psychology.* Vol. 7 of *The collected works of C. G. Jung*, 2nd ed. Translated by R. F. C. Hull. Princeton, N.J.: Princeton University Press, Bollingen Series XX.

———. 1968a. *Aion, Researches into the phenomenology of the self.* Vol. 9, part 2 of *The collected works of C. G. Jung*, 2nd ed. Translated by R. F. C. Hull. Princeton, N.J.: Princeton University Press, Bollingen Series XX.

———. 1968b. *Psychology and alchemy.* Vol. 12 of *The collected works of C. G. Jung*, 2nd ed. Translated by R. F. C. Hull. Princeton, N.J.: Princeton University Press, Bollingen Series XX.

Kadloubovsky, E. and G. E. H. Palmer., eds. and trans. 1954. *Early fathers from the Philokalia.* London and Boston: Faber.

Kavanaugh, K. and O. Rodriquez, trans. 1980. *The Collected Works of St. Teresa of Avila*, vol. 2. Washington, D.C.: ICS Publications.

Kazantzakis, N. 1952. *Zorba the Greek.* Translated by C. Waldman. New York: Simon & Schuster.

———. 1960a. *The last temptation of Christ.* Translated by P. A. Bien. New York: Simon & Schuster.

———. 1960b. *The saviors of God: Spiritual exercises.* Translated by K. Friar. New York: Simon & Schuster.

———. 1962. *Saint Francis.* Translated by P. A. Bien. New York: Simon & Schuster.

———. 1965. *Report to Greco.* Translated by P. A. Bien. New York: Simon & Schuster.

Kelsey, M. T. 1976. *The other side of silence: A guide to Christian meditation.* New York: Paulist.

Kerényi, C. 1951. *The gods of the Greeks.* Translated by N. Cameron. London: Thames & Hudson.

———. 1976. *Dionysos: Archetypal image of indestructible life.* Translated by R. Manheim. Vol. 2 of *Archetypal images in Greek religion.* Princeton, N.J.: Princeton University Press.

Kiefer, O. 1953. *Sexual life in ancient Rome.* Translated by G. and H. Highet. New York: Barnes & Noble.

Lamb, F. B. 1974. *Wizard of the upper Amazon: The story of Manuel Córdova-Rios*, 2nd ed. Boston: Houghton Mifflin.

Lawrence, D. H. 1966. *Apocalypse.* New York: Viking Press.

———. 1976. *Women in love.* Middlesex, Eng.: Penguin.

Leakey, R. E. and R. Lewin. 1977. *Origins: What new discoveries reveal about the emergence of our species and its possible future.* New York: Dutton.

Lorenz, K. 1966. *On aggression.* Translated by M. K. Wilson. New York: Bantam.

Lowen, A. 1967. *The betrayal of the body.* New York: Collier.

———. 1970. *Pleasure: A creative approach to life.* Middlesex, Eng.: Penguin.

———. 1972. *Depression and the body: The biological basis of faith and reality.* Baltimore, Md.: Penguin.

————. 1976. *Bioenergetics.* Middlesex, Eng.: Penguin.

Lunde, D. T. July, 1975. Our murder boom. *Psychology Today,* 35–42.

McClinton, K. M. 1962. *Christian church art through the ages.* New York: Macmillan.

Montagu, A., ed. 1973. *Man and aggression,* 2nd ed. London: Oxford University Press.

Moore, R. and D. Gillette. 1990. *King, warrior, magician, lover: Rediscovering the archetypes of the mature masculine.* New York: HarperCollins.

Morris, D. 1968. *The naked ape.* New York: McGraw-Hill.

Neumann, E. 1954. *The origins and history of consciousness.* Translated by R. F. C. Hull. Princeton, N.J.: Princeton University Press.

————. 1963. *The great mother: An analysis of the archetype,* 2nd ed. Princeton, N.J.: Princeton University Press.

New English Bible. 1971. New York: Cambridge University Press.

Nietzsche, F. 1954. *The portable Nietzsche.* Translated by W. Kaufmann. New York: Viking.

Pennington, M. B. 1980. *Centering prayer: Renewing an ancient Christian prayer form.* Garden City, N.Y.: Doubleday.

Perera, S. B. 1981. *Descent to the goddess: A way of initiation for women.* Toronto: Inner City.

Quispel, G. 1979. *The secret book of Revelation: The last book of the Bible.* New York: McGraw-Hill.

Randall, J. H., Jr. 1940. *The making of the modern mind: A survey of the intellectual background of the present age,* rev. ed. Cambridge, Mass.: Houghton Mifflin.

Radha, Swami S. 1978. *Kundalini: Yoga for the West.* Spokane, Wash.: Timeless.

Ram Dass. 1978. *Journey of awakening: A meditator's guidebook.* New York: Bantam.

Rodriguez, O. and K. Kavanaugh, trans. 1980. *The collected works of St. Teresa of Avila,* vol. 2. Washington, D.C.: ICS Publications.

Saggs, H. W. F. 1962. *The greatness that was Babylon: A sketch of the ancient civilization of the Tigris-Euphrates valley.* New York: Hawthorn books.

Schwab, G. 1946. *Gods & heroes: Myths and epics of ancient Greece.* New York: Pantheon.

Scull, C. S. 1989. Existential themes in interviews with Vietnam veterans. Ph.D. diss. Institute of Transpersonal Psychology, Palo Alto, Calif.

Singer, J. 1973. *Boundaries of the soul: The practice of Jung's psychology.* Garden City, N.Y.: Anchor.

————. 1977. *Androgyny: Toward a new theory of sexuality.* Garden City, N.Y.: Anchor.

Smith, H. 1991. *The world's religions.* San Francisco: HarperSanFrancisco.

Speiser, E. A. 1964. *The Anchor Bible, Genesis.* Garden City, N.Y.: Doubleday.

Teilhard de Chardin, P. 1969. *Building the earth and the psychological conditions of human unification.* Translated by N. Lindsay. New York: Avon.

Thompson, K. 1982. What men really want: A *New Age* interview with Robert Bly. *New Age (May 1982):* 30–36, 50–51.

Underhill, E. 1961. *Mysticism: A study in the nature and development of man's spiritual consciousness.* New York: Dutton.

Vaughan, F. 1986. *The inward arc: Healing and wholeness in psychotherapy and spirituality.* Boston: Shambhala.

Voegelin, E. 1956. *Israel and revelation.* Vol. 1 of *Order and History.* Baton Rouge, La.: Louisiana State University Press.

von Franz, M.-L. 1964. The process of individuation. In C. G. Jung, ed. *Man and his symbols,* 159–254. New York: Dell.

von Rad, G. 1962. *The theology of Israel's historical traditions.* Vol. 1 of *Old Testament theology.* New York: Harper & Row.

Ward, G. 1992. Douglas MacArthur: An American soldier. *National Geographic,* 181, no. 3 (March 1992): 54–83.

Whitmont, E. 1982. *The return of the goddess.* New York: Crossroad.

Wilber, K. 1980. *The atman project: A transpersonal view of human development,* Wheaton, Ill.: Theosophical.

———. 1981a. *No boundary, Eastern and Western approaches to personal growth.* Boulder and London: Shambhala.

———. 1981b. *Up from Eden: A transpersonal view of human evolution.* Garden City, N.Y., Anchor.

———, ed. 1982. *The holographic paradigm and other paradoxes: Exploring the leading edge of science.* Boulder and London: Shambhala.

Woolger, J. and R. 1989. *The goddess within: A guide to eternal myths that shape women's lives.* New York: Fawcett.

Workman, H. B. 1962. *The evolution of the monastic ideal.* Boston: Beacon.